The Revived Roman Empire

Europe In Bible Prophecy

ERIKA GREY

Pedante Press

Danbury, CT

Pe Danté Press™

The Revived Roman Empire: Europe in Bible Prophecy
Copyright © 2013 Erika Grey
All rights reserved.

No Part of this publication may be reproduced in any form without written permission from Pedante Press.

Pedante Press
Suite #4 White Oak
Danbury, CT 06810

Library of Congress Control Number: 2013949092
Grey, Erika
The Revived Roman Empire: Europe In Bible Prophecy /Erika Grey
p. cm.

ISBN: 978-0-9790199-7-5
ISBN: -0-9790199-7-4

ABOUT THIS REPORT

In this report, I teamed up with teamed up with Global Watch Weekly (Rema Marketing) to produce The Revived Roman Empire. They provided the introductory material on the history of the Roman Empire, the detailed expose on Pope Benedict, photos and cited Media Alert articles. I provided all of the material on the EU and Bible Prophecy.

For ERIKA GREY'S
Books & Articles
www.erikagrey.com

CONTENTS

	Introduction	i
1	The Biblical Basis For a Revived Roman Empire	1
2	From Ancient Rome Until World War I	5
3	Holy Roman Empire Architects	17
4	Forging a Catholic Europe	23
5	Babylonian Europe	33
6	Political Power: The Basis of The New Order	41
7	Pope Francis: The Jesuit Conduit	55
8	The Return of The Empire	61
9	Building an Empire	75
10	The EU And The Nations of The World	91
11	The Thrones of Europe	95
12	The Antichrist	107
13	The EU Technology Agenda	115
14	The EU-US Partnership	129
15	Confirming The Covenant	146
16	The Final World Empire And God's Promise	167

INTRODUCTION

The belief that there is any prophetical relevance to the rise of the European Union and its chaotic quest for political unity has come under severe fire over the last decade. From the Treaty of Rome in 1957 to the Maastricht Treaty in 1991 and the Lisbon Treaty of 2004 instead of history witnessing the emergence of a 21st century super power, we have only seen absolute chaos as member nations such as Greece, Italy, Spain, Portugal, Ireland and even more recently, Cyprus, plummeting into a financial precipice destroying the reputation and credibility of the European Union in the process.

Many bible prophecy researchers have used this as leverage to introduce alternative views regarding the final super power from which the Antichrist will emerge. Should we forget about the European Union? Is it really a failed experiment of the Club of Rome that has failed to live up to expectation? Is the European Union simply a toothless entity trying to justify its global prowess in a world where the power dynamics are changing?

Yet the idea of a united Europe is more than just a quest for economic stability and prosperity. It is a long- standing vision that has captured the imagination of intellectuals who have wanted something to believe in as they attempt to build a better world. European unification was devised as a way to eliminate war from the continent. By tying the countries of Europe together with common laws, a common currency, a European Court, a Central Bank and a host of other intertwined institutions, Europe's planners hoped to keep age-old rivalries from resurfacing and tearing Europe apart. But is the unification of Europe the pathway to a peaceful future-or is it a nightmare in the making?

This report uncovers the power structures of the European Union and provides a geopolitical framework for understanding the development of the European Union and how the evidence proves that it fits the biblical requirement for a revival of the Roman Empire.

The Revived Roman Empire identifies the European Union as the final world empire, which will launch the Antichrist. In addition, the reader discovers the relationship between the ancient prophetic writings, the European Union and today's current affairs. No report dealing with Bible Prophecy provides such in-depth analysis and extensive research as The Revived Roman Empire, which presents the reader with a gripping, riveting expose in line with the present geopolitical framework.

1

THE BIBLICAL BASIS FOR A REVIVED ROMAN EMPIRE

Finally, there will be a fourth kingdom, strong as iron-for iron breaks and smashes everything-and as iron breaks things to pieces, so it will crush and break all the others. 41 Just as you saw that the feet and toes were partly of baked clay and partly of iron, so this will be a divided kingdom; yet it will have some of the strength of iron in it, even as you saw iron mixed with clay. 42 As the toes were partly iron and partly clay, so this kingdom will be partly strong and partly brittle. And just as you saw the iron mixed with baked clay, so the people will be a mixture and will not remain united, any more than iron mixes with clay (Daniel 2:40-43).

THE BIBLICAL BASIS FOR A REVIVED ROMAN EMPIRE

The basis for the belief that there is a connection between the European Union and the biblical prophecies of a final end time a revived Roman Empire is based predominantly on Daniel 2. This passage of scripture outlines that there would be four world empires that would arise on the world scene from the time of Daniels vision until the second coming of Christ. Whilst there have been other world empires which have existed other than these four, the common denominator is that these would be four empires which would control and have power the nation of Israel.

Daniel confirmed in his interpretation that the first empire represented by the head of gold was in reference to Babylon which at that time was under the rule of Nebuchadnezzar. Babylon would then be succeeded by the Medes and Persian (symbolized by arms and chest of silver) which in turn would be dominated by Greece (thighs of brass). Ultimately the fourth and final world empire would be the Roman Empire which succeeded Greece but this Roman Empire would have two periods of existence. Firstly, immediately following the decline of the Grecian Empire but then again in a time period preceding the second Coming of Christ since the later existence of a deteriorated Roman Empire is linked to the coming of Christ and the establishment of his kingdom on earth.

So it is important to lay the foundation by making reference to Dr. John Walvoord one of the great prophecy scholars of the 20th century who provides an exegesis of Daniel 2 which forms the basis of this report.

In the prophecies of Daniel, especially Daniel 2, prophetically four world empires are set forth. In the image of Daniel 2 the head of gold is related to Babylon by practically all expositors. Most expositors also recognize three other empires in the shoulders of silver (Medo-Persia), the lower part of the body of bronze (Grecian Empire), and the legs of iron (Roman Empire) and the feet part of iron and part of clay (fulfillment in a revival of a last days Roman Empire) The significance and recurring theme of ten is also found in The following scriptural passages (Dan 2:34-35, 40-45; 7:7-8, 19-24 ; Rev 13:1-2; 17:3, 7,

12-16) which demonstrate that a future ten-nation confederacy in the Middle East will form a large part in prophecy of the end time and be the forerunner of the ultimate world government.

The question of whether the ancient Roman Empire will be revived in the prophetic future at the end of the age is one of the intriguing interpretative problems of the Scriptures. In the twentieth century the question of the revival of Rome has taken on new prominence with the revival of the Middle East as a whole, the formation of the new State of Israel, the reformations of the Roman Catholic Church, and many other factors which again are directing attention to the Middle East. Accordingly, the revival of Rome becomes once again a live question.

The two legs of the image of Daniel 2, likewise, portray the eastern and western divisions of the Roman Empire. The unequal duration of the eastern empire, which continued long after the western empire had fallen apart, is not seen in Daniel's prophecy because it occurs in the period of the present church age which does not seem to be in Daniel's fore view. The unfulfilled aspects of the prophecies provide the clue for the future revival of Rome. Any other view has never achieved majority status among evangelicals at least because the prophecies taken literally lead to this conclusion.

If the large discussion available in evangelical literature supports the conclusion that the fourth empire of Daniel was Roman, the question remains whether its future revival will also be Roman, and whether the Scriptures specifically teach this. The ten-nation confederacy is anticipated in the feet-stage of the image, and although the toes are not said to be ten in number, this is the implication. More specific details are given in Daniel on the fourth beast of his vision in chapter 7. There in the latter stage of development the beast is declared to have ten horns. This is interpreted in Daniel 7:24 as "ten kings that shall arise." Further light is cast on this in Revelation 13 where a beast is seen to come out of the sea having "ten horns." The fact that the ten-horns stage of the kingdom was still prophetic when the book of Revelation was written clearly makes it either Roman or post-Roman in its historical fulfillment.

The ten-nation confederacy of the future anticipated in these prophecies would naturally be considered a revival of the Roman Empire if for no other reason than that it is portrayed as an integral part of the fourth empire. As far as Daniel and Revelation are concerned, there is no sharp break between the historic and the prophetic, and the present age in which the church is being called out from Jew and Gentile alike is not taken into consideration in Daniel's fore view. Accordingly, the fourth empire of the past and the future confederacy are looked upon as if they are parts of the same empire. If the fourth empire is Roman, it would follow that the ten-nation confederacy will also be Roman in character, at least from the divine point of view.

A second argument in favor of the identification of the future empire as Roman would come from the geographic evidence that the center of the stage is the Middle East in the end of the age. It is here that the great final world war is fought according to Daniel 11:36-45, confirmed by the reference to

Armageddon in Revelation 16:16, and other geographic indications such as the River Euphrates, the city of Jerusalem, and similar geographic factors. If the future activities relating to the ten-nation confederacy are in the Middle East, it would also support the concept that it is a revival of the ancient Roman Empire, at least geographically.

One of the most specific references, however, is found in the difficult prophecy of Daniel in which Israel's history is unfolded as recorded in Daniel 9:24-27. One of the important factors in this prophecy is Daniel 9:26 where it is stated that after the Messiah or the Anointed One is cut off that "the people of the prince that shall come shall destroy the city and the sanctuary." Although there have been many destructions of Jerusalem, most commentators agree that the fulfillment of this prophecy was in A.D. 70 when the Roman General Titus surrounded the city of Jerusalem, slaughtered its inhabitants, and burned the beautiful temple whose construction had been completed only six years before. If this prince is the same as the little horn (Dan 7:8), who subdues three of the ten nations in the confederacy and assumes control, it would follow from this that the prince who will come, because of his relation to the people who destroyed the city in A.D. 70, will be a Roman prince. This view is far preferable to the interpretation of "the prince that shall come" as a reference to Christ.

Although this does not establish his racial background, and debate continues as to his particular nationality, politically he will be the final ruler of Roman power in the world until the second coming of Jesus Christ. Accordingly, many expositors identify the prince that shall come as the ultimate world ruler mentioned in Revelation 13 and other passages.

That this is related to end-time events, and therefore either Roman or post-Roman, is confirmed by the reference in the Olivet Discourse where Christ cited the abomination of desolation, prophesied in Daniel 9:27, as being the sign of the beginning of the great tribulation. In the context, Christ relates this to Judea and again fixes the center of events as being in the Middle East. Accordingly, on the basis of the prophecy of Christ and the future anticipations of Revelation 13, the liberal contention that all of this was fulfilled in the second century B.C. becomes completely untenable. In making the prophecy of Matthew 24, Christ also confirms the prophetic accuracy of Daniel, and takes the prediction of the future abomination of desolation, which refers to the desecration of a future temple in Jerusalem, as a literal event of great significance to the people of Israel.

On the basis of the conclusion that the fourth empire of Daniel is Roman, that geographically the future ten-nation confederacy is in the area occupied in history by the Roman Empire, and the specific reference to the prince that shall come as being related to the Roman people, a conclusion can be drawn that there will be a revival of Rome politically, which will fulfill the unfulfilled aspect of the fourth empire, both in Daniel and in Revelation.

2

FROM ANCIENT ROME UNTIL WORLD WAR I

The Holy Roman Empire was an attempt to revive the Western Roman Empire, whose legal and political structure deteriorated during the 5th and 6th centuries, to be replaced by independent kingdoms ruled by Germanic nobles. The Roman imperial office was vacant after the deposition of Romulus Augustulus in 476. During the turbulent early Middle Ages the traditional concept of a temporal realm coextensive with the spiritual realm of the church had been kept alive by the popes in Rome. Hundreds of years later in the early stages of the twentieth century the region of Europe after World War I again faced a political vacuum for which history would then again repeat itself.

THE EARLY CHURCH AND THE ROMAN EMPIRE

The Roman Empire like Babylon, Medo-Persia and Greece eventually began to decline after being in power for over years. During the time that the Roman Empire had been in existence the early Church of the Acts had become the dominant Christian denomination despite the fact that early on in her history the church had come under tremendous persecution from imperial Rome. The first recorded official persecution of Christians on behalf of the Roman Empire was in 64 AD, when, as reported by the Roman historian Tacitus, Emperor Nero blamed Christians for the Great Fire of Rome. According to Church tradition, it was during the reign of Nero that Peter and Paul were martyred in Rome.

Christians suffered from sporadic and localized persecutions over a period of two and a half centuries. Their refusal to participate in Imperial cult was considered an act of treason and was thus punishable by execution. The most widespread official persecution was carried out by Diocletian. During the Great Persecution (303-311), the emperor ordered Christian buildings and the homes of Christians torn down and their sacred books collected and burned. Christians were arrested, tortured, mutilated, burned, starved, and condemned to gladiatorial contests to amuse spectators. The Great Persecution officially ended in April 311, when Galerius, senior emperor of the Tetrarchy, issued an edict of toleration, which granted Christians the right to practice their religion, though it did not restore any property to them.

However it was during the rule of Roman Emperor Constantine the Great (reigned 306-337) that Christianity became a dominant religion of the Roman Empire. Historians remain uncertain about Constantine's reasons for favoring Christianity, and theologians and historians have argued about which form of Christianity he subscribed to. Constantine's conversion was a turning point for Early Christianity, sometimes referred to as the Triumph of the Church, the Peace of the Church or the Constantinian shift. In 313, Constantine and Licinius issued the Edict of Milan legalizing Christian worship. The emperor became a great patron of the Church and set a precedent for the position of the Christian emperor within the Church and the notion of orthodoxy, Christendom, ecumenical councils and the state church of the Roman Empire declared by edict in 380 AD.

However the power of the church took an extraordinary turn in 391AD when Ambrose the bishop of Milan convinced the Roman Emperor Theodosius to outlaw all of the religions in the Roman Empire except for the Roman Church. Romulus Augustus (born perhaps around 460 - died after 476, possibly alive around 500), is sometimes considered the last Western Roman Emperor (although by other accounts the last Western Roman Emperor was Julius Nepos), reigning from 31 October 475 until 4 September 476. His deposition by Odoacer traditionally marks the end of the Western Roman Empire, the fall of ancient Rome, and the beginning of the Middle Ages in Western Europe. After the fall of the Western Roman Empire in 476, the Catholic faith competed with Arianism for the conversion of the barbarian tribes.

Early in the fifth century the Merovingian's established themselves in what is now Belgium and northern France. There they adopted the Cabalistic pseudo-Christianity of the Cathars, a dualistic religion that holds there are two eternal gods, the god of Good and the god of Evil. Under Clovis I the pagan King of the Franks, who reigned from 481-511, the Franks converted to Roman Catholicism in AD496. Through him, Rome began to establish undisputed supremacy in Western Europe. In return for being the sword of Rome whereby the church would manifest her power and impose a spiritual dominion, Clovis was granted the title of "New Constantine" and to preside over a unified "Holy Roman Empire" based on the church and administered on the secular level in perpetuity by the Merovingian bloodline. Like "the sure mercies of David", this was a pact that could be modified, but not revoked, broken or betrayed.

The Merovingian's believed that Jesus survived the cross and married Mary Magdalene who bore his son then lived in seclusion in the south of France. During the fifth century this lineage is said to have married with the royal line of the Franks engendering the Merovingian dynasty. When in 496 the church pledged itself in perpetuity to the Merovingian bloodline it was presumably in full knowledge of their claimed identity. This would explain why Clovis was offered the status of Holy Roman Emperor, and why he was not created but only "crowned" king. The title that Clovis and his descendants were originally given by the Pope when the covenant between the Vatican and the Merovingian's first began in 496 A.D. was "New Constantine", giving him secular authority over the choicest bits of Christian Europe, just like the authority which the namesake of the office, Constantine, had once enjoyed.

But Constantine had been the "thirteenth apostle", and was responsible for the incorporation of Christianity into the Roman institution. He was therefore also a priest-king, holding spiritual dominion as well as secular dominion, just as previous Roman emperors had done.

But when the later Merovingian kings began to exhibit a desire to exercise their own spiritual authority, which rested partially upon the foundation of their claimed blood relationship to Jesus Christ and King David, it sparked a chain of events that culminated in the assassination of Dagobert II, the last effective Merovingian king, and the loss of the title "New Constantine" for his descendants. However, the Merovingian's appear to have taken their right to the title, and their right to European hegemony, very seriously, in a manner that seems to be rooted in something more ancient than the time of Clovis. They believe, perhaps because of their descent from Christ and King David that they were already entitled to rule over Europe long before it was sanctioned by the Pope.

This "Divine Right" was recognized by their loyal subjects as well, who regarded the Merovingian's as semi-divine priest-kings, and who formed a cult worshipping Dagobert II after his death. With a following like that, the Merovingian's were not about to give up their rightful inheritance without a fight.

Less than 200 years later, a man named Charlemagne (Charles the Great), who married a Merovingian princess, was made Holy Roman Emperor, and given dominion over a land mass greater even than that which the Merovingian's had possessed. Thus began the majestic Carolingian dynasty, consisting after Charlemagne of men with partially Merovingian blood. Charlemagne too was considered a priest-king, and is probably the most famous and beloved figure in French history.

And while he may not have ruled over the entire world in actuality, he did have dominion over its most significant portion. For at that time Western Europe was without a doubt the foremost bastion of culture, science, philosophy, and morality, a light in the darkness, surrounded on all fronts by uncivilized barbarian hordes.

THE REVIVED ROMAN EMPIRE: Europe In Bible Prophecy

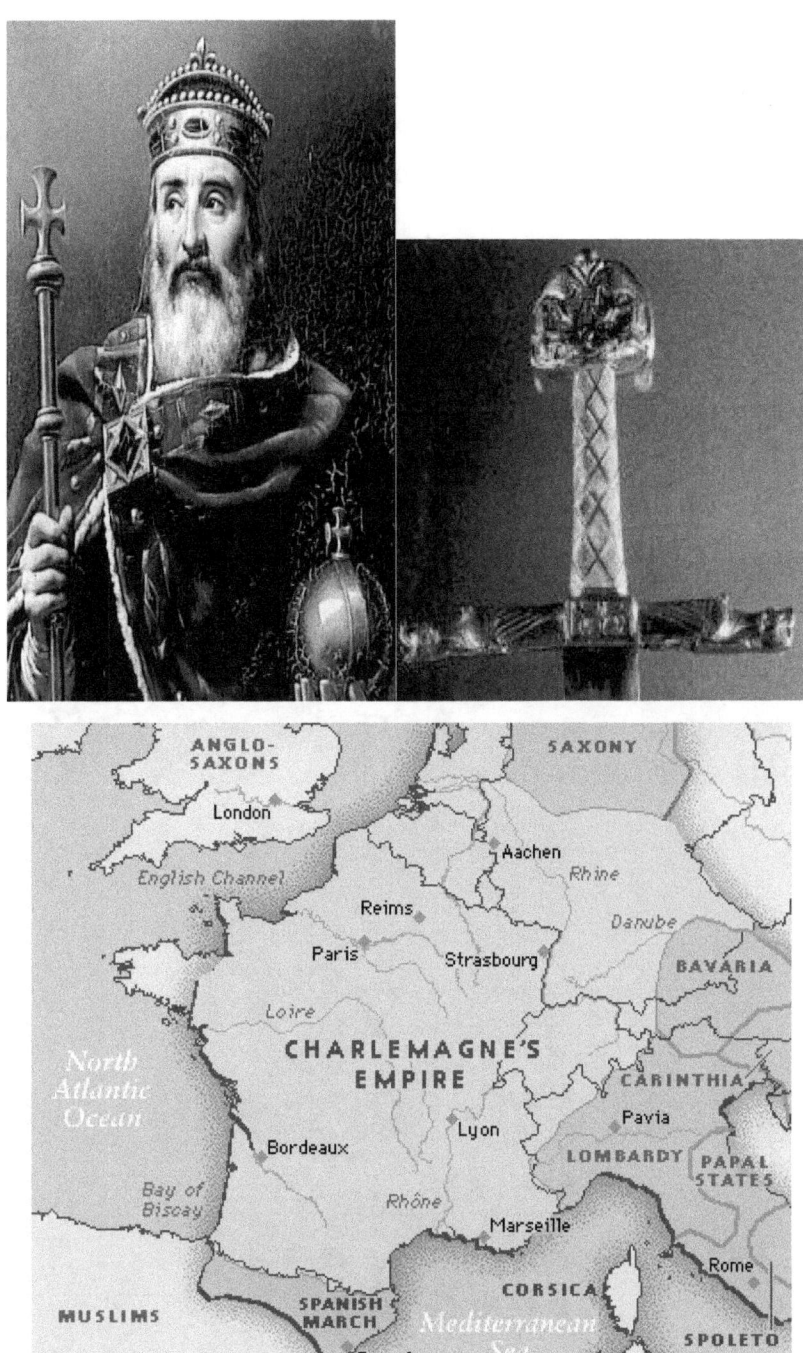

The Carolingian dynasty ended in 918, but the Holy Roman Empire continued to play a decisive role in the unfolding of its destiny. It was during this time that the Empire began to turn its sights towards the Holy Land. The first Crusade began in 1095, and the entire enterprise was brought about because of the pressure that certain Merovingian descendants placed upon the Pope and the nobility of Europe.

This resulted in the capture of Jerusalem four years later, and the creation of the Latin Kingdom of Jerusalem as part of the Holy Roman Empire. The capture was lead by Godfroi de Bouillon, a descendant of Dagobert II, and his brother, Baldwin I, was proclaimed King of Jerusalem. The

Merovingian descendants appear to have considered the Holy Land their rightful possession, once again due to their direct descent from King David, and Jerusalem was in a way their coronation stone, legitimizing their eventual return to the rule of the Holy Roman Empire.

It was to this goal that they immediately dedicated themselves, and with the help of Baldwin II (son of Baldwin I, who died shortly after the capture of the Holy Land), a group of Knights was formed supposedly to help keep the roads to Jerusalem safe for pilgrims. Its core members were all from the Merovingian "Grail families", and they soon went about establishing their own sort of empire throughout Europe - one based upon the power of money.

The Knight Templars were legally beholden to none but the Pope, and even that they took lightly, so any land controlled by them was essentially an independent principality. They held possessions throughout the continent, and controlled major industries, especially that of banking. Soon, they had all the princes of Europe indebted to them. It took the Pope and the King of France colluding against them to get them disbanded, excommunicated, and in some cases burnt at the stake before the Templar menace was finally subdued. Meanwhile, Merovingian descendants were busy reclaiming the throne of the Holy Roman Empire via another avenue. In 1273, Count Rudolf of the Merovingian-entwined Habsburg dynasty (later Habsburg-Lorraine) was elected Holy Roman Emperor, and the title stayed within the family until the Empire itself collapsed in 1806.

The Holy Roman Empire actually persisted into the early 19th century. At this time it was centralized in the loosely defined and allied Germanic states/kingdoms. Following the rise of Napoleon and the defeat of many different, unaligned German kingdoms' forces by Napoleon's forces, Napoleon was able to sweep across the nation we now know as Germany. One of the first things Napoleon did was to dismantle the once-proud Holy Roman Empire as well as install a number of administrative and economic reforms. Doing so actually laid the foundations of a (loose) sense of German nationalism that had not existed prior to this and led the way to many of the revolutionary happenings of the 19th century in central Europe (more specifically in Germany, Prussia, Hungary, Austria, Denmark, France, and many other tiny German principalities and duchies).

Interestingly, Napoleon, himself husband of a Merovingian princess who had consciously attempted to associate himself with the Merovingian mystique by placing golden bees from the tomb of Merovingian King Childeric III on his coronation robe. It is also interesting to note that, although he was not of royal blood himself, he was recognized as an emperor, and ruled over a pan-European empire much like the one that he had just crushed.

MEDIA INSIGHT (DAILYMAIL.CO.UK)
END OF A ROYAL DYNASTY: OTTO VON HABSBURG LAID TO REST

Otto von Habsburg's death officially marks the end of a 640-year dynasty of Europe's once most powerful royal family that supplied the continent with a nearly uninterrupted stream of rulers. Also spelled Hapsburg, the name came from the castle of Habichtsburg, meaning Hawk's Castle, built in the 11th century in Switzerland.

The family can be traced back to the 10th century and it established a hereditary monarchy in Austria in the 13th century. From 1452 it held the title of Holy Roman Emperor almost continuously until the empire was dissolved by Napoleon in 1806. It reached its greatest extent in the early 16th century under Charles V, who, through diplomacy, marriage, and conquest, ruled one of the largest empires ever created. In addition to its heartland in central Europe, it included Spain, the kingdom of Naples and other parts of Italy, and most of the Netherlands, as well as vast colonial possessions in the Americas.

When Charles abdicated in 1556 the empire was divided between his son Philip, who inherited Spain, the New World colonies, the Italian possessions, and the Netherlands, and his brother Ferdinand, who inherited the rest (the 'Austrian' territories), as well as the title of emperor. The Habsburgs ruled in Spain until 1700 and in Austria until 1918, when the upheavals of the First World War brought the dynasty to an end.

Otto von Habsburg, whose full name was Franz Joseph Otto Robert Maria Anton Karl Max Heinrich Sixtus Xavier Felix Renatus Ludwig Gaetan Pius Ignatius von Habsburg, was born in 1912 in Reichenau, Austria. He became crown prince when his father, Charles I, was crowned emperor in 1916, during World War I. After Austria and Germany lost World War I, the Austria-Hungarian Empire was dismantled, Charles I had to abdicate and Austria went on to become a republic. While never formally renouncing his right to the throne, Habsburg in his later life became an outspoken supporter of parliamentary democracy and a fighter for a united Europe.

With the 1989 fall of the Berlin Wall, Habsburg used his seat in European Parliament to lobby for expanding the European Union to include former Eastern bloc nations. He was a member of the European Parliament for the conservative Bavarian Christian Social Union in southern Germany and also served as president of the Pan-European League from 1979 to 1999. Karl, the eldest son of Otto and Regina Habsburg, now runs the family's affairs and has been the official head of the House of Habsburg since 2007.

The Habsburgs remained the emperors of Austria, and then Austro- Hungary, until the revolution of 1919, making them the longest reigning European dynasty in history. And their role in European politics wasn't over as evidenced by Otto Von Habsburgs influence as we see shortly. Notably despite the overthrow of the Holy Roman Empire by Napoleon the Roman Catholic Church and Popes still continued to exist albeit with reduced authority. With the overthrow of Catholic Church as a political power and no longer having the military protection it had enjoyed for thousands of year prior, the church had no ability to resist when King Victor Emmanuel II of Sardinia was proclaimed King of Italy. The state was founded as a result of the unification of Italy under the influence of the Kingdom of Sardinia, which was its legal predecessor state. However between 1861 and 1929, the Vatican City refused to recognize the Italian King's reign over the city, and the question of whether the Pope was in charge or the King was referred to as the Roman Question. This was eventually resolved upon independence of Vatican State as a separate country from Italy and ever since the Roman Catholic Church leads the city-state.

With the overthrow of the Holy Roman Empire leading to a vacuum in which Rome's grip had finally been cut loose. It took only 67 years from the end of the Holy Roman Empire for the Merovingian Grail families to begin jockeying once again for control of Europe. The Knights Templar had been the brainchild of another secret society which spawned them: the Priory of Sion, an order dedicated to nothing less than the restoration of the Merovingian bloodline to the thrones of Europe. And in 1873, they sponsored the creation of another front organization - the Hieron du Val d'Or, whose name, as the book Holy Blood, Holy Grail notes, contains an anagram of the place-name "Orval", a location that seems to be particularly important to the Merovingian's and the Priory of Sion. Notably, the word "Orval" contains the syllables which, in French, mean "gold" and "valley." Thus "Val d'Or" means "Valley of Gold."

In his 1979 book Le Tresor du Triangle d'Or (The Treasure of the Golden Triangle), Jean-Luc Chaumeil states that the Hieron practiced a version of Scottish Rite Freemasonry, and that the upper degrees of this order constituted the lower degrees of the Priory of Sion itself. Chaumeil described the group's disposition as "Christian, Hermetic, and aristocratic."

They proclaimed themselves to be Catholic, even though the Church of Rome condemned them. Their mystic teachings contained, according to Holy Blood, Holy Grail, "a characteristic emphasis on sacred geometry and various sacred sites... an insistence on a mystical or Gnostic truth underlying mythological motifs", and "a preoccupation with the origins of men, races, languages, and symbols... "

The order was, "simultaneously Christian and 'trans-Christian.' It stressed the importance of the Sacred Heart... sought to recognize Christian and pagan mysteries... [and]... Ascribed special significance to Druidic thought - which it... regarded as partially Pythagorean."

The Hieron du Val d'Or was also unabashedly pro-monarchist, and sought a restoration of the Holy Roman Empire. But this one would be built, unlike the previous one, on an ultimately spiritual basis – a vision specifically echoed in the Priory of Sion's own literature. The new empire would have been a reflection of Heaven on Earth, that specifically Hermetic Arcadian ideal. Jean-Luc Chaumeil described the Hieron's agenda as: "...a theocracy wherein nations would be no more than provinces, their leaders but proconsuls in the service of a world occult government consisting of an elite. For Europe, this regime of the Great King implied a double hegemony of the Papacy and the Empire, of the Vatican and of the Habsburgs, who would have been the Vatican's right arm."

The events surrounding World War I toppled the Western monarchies, and for the first half of this century Europe was in total chaos. It seemed impossible for current events to be any more out of sync with the goals of the Merovingian bloodline during that time. But the chaos worked to their advantage, because it created the need for a new European order (for which the Priory of Sion, the Hieron du Val d'Or took full advantage of) an order from which the embryonic form of the European Union would eventually arise. It also created the opportunity for the Roman Catholic Church to again exert its influence on the direction of the Europe.

During this period of European vacuum Otto von Habsburg was not content to allow his family tradition of European unity to die and founded the European Center of Documentation and Information (CEDI),51 whose objective was to construct around the Spanish Borb6ns a federation of European states united in Christianity and anti-Communism.

This sounded very much like a modern resurrection of the Holy Roman Empire over which Charles V had reigned. Like the Spanish empire of old, the envisaged Catholic federation was intended to have large- spectrum antennae in Latin America and the United States. Otto von Habsburg had also been named as a member of the Order of Malta, a member of Opus Dei, and a member of the Mont Pelerin Society (a branch of the Pan Europa Union).

Possibly von Habsburg's most controversial suggestion has been his recipe for dealing with national emergencies. In the April 1978 issue of his conservative publication Zeitbuhne, he suggested that in certain emergency situations (such as nuclear blackmail or other major acts of terrorism) "governments should let a strongman take over for a period of nine months, allowing him to suspend laws and 'take all measure necessary for the maintenance of the life of the population."

Christopher Hollis, in the foreword to von Habsburg's book The Social Order of Tomorrow, points out that Otto 'wanted to see Europe resume her essential unity, and in the symbolism of that unity he thinks that the imperial crown of Charlemagne and of the Holy Roman Empire might well have its part to play.'

"Inter-European unity has long been a quest of the Habsburg dynasty. Otto himself often speaks of the similarities between the Holy Roman Empire of the Middle Ages and his view of a coming United States of Europe."

In this regard, Otto had stressed the importance of religion in the formation of a united Europe. He regards Christianity as Europe's bulwark: "The cross doesn't need Europe, but Europe needs the cross." For centuries before, the ruling Habsburgs defended the Continent against the expansion of the Turkish Ottoman Empire and Mr. von Habsburg makes it clear that all nations bordering the Mediterranean Sea - including those in North Africa and the Middle East (the Islamic states) - had a place in his broad vision for tomorrow's Europe. A very significant statement considering what we see happening today with the European Union's policy towards the Middle East and North Africa.

Otto von Habsburg was also president of the Pan Europa Union50 from 1973-2004. The Pan European Movement is a supranational organization founded in 1923 by Count Richard Coudenhove-Kalergi whose goal was the unity of Europe. Although the Pan European Movement is independent of all political parties, it holds clear and well-defined principles by which it appraises politicians, parties and institutions. The four main basic principles are based on liberalism, Christianity social responsibility, and pro- Europeanism. However its more controversial position has included keeping Moscow out of Europe and creating a Roman Catholic-oriented European Superstate. The Union also believed that that Britain should be kept out of Pan Europa since it manages an autonomous empire. Unlike Russia, Turkey belonged to Asia and also should not be included in Pan Europa, according to Kalergi. The Pan European Union is also responsible for the 12 stars on a blue ground as official symbol for Europe, which symbolizes the stars of the Virgin Mary. This flag was the basis by which the European Union flag was eventually created and it still the symbol used in its meetings today (see below president of EU Council, Herman Von Rompuy at the annual Pan Europa Meeting)

Before his death in 2011, Otto Von Habsburg the great bastion for European unity in the 20th century had the opportunity to meet Pope John Paul II and Pope Benedict in meetings which would symbolize the meeting of Charlemagne and Pope Pius III in AD 800. The convergence of political and spiritual Rome, a symbolism alluded to in Revelation 17 as a union between the beast and the harlot; the ultimate Bab

3

HOLY ROMAN EMPIRE ARCHITECHTS

The European Union flag is dark blue and has 12 stars in a circle. In a Dutch, Catholic periodical, Middelares en Koningin, April, 1974, we find the headline: "Under the Protection of Mary". It says among other things: "We Catholics will always, when we see the blue color, perceive it as the color of the Queen of Heaven" (it is also called Mary-blue). On the imprint of the new Euro we also find 12 stars on both coins and paper money. No matter how many members the EU will consist of, there will always be 12 stars. Why just 12 stars? Why not the number of membership countries? Much indicates that the 12-star circle on the European Union flag took its inspiration from the worship of Mary in the Catholic Church. In the Catholic Church, the Queen of Heaven, Mary, with the 12 stars around her head, is a well-known motif. The acceptance of the flag of Europe took place on the very day of the 101st anniversary of Pope Pius IX's doctrine of Mary's Immaculate Conception, December 8, 1854. The European Council's receiving of the "Mary flag" on that day was hardly a coincidence.

"The relationship between church and state is described in the Scriptures as one of "fornication" (Revelation 17:2). Unlike marriage where two people give themselves to each other, a relationship of fornication between a man and a woman is a selfish one, with each trying to get from the other. This is exactly how the relationship has been between the church and the secular European leaders down through history, each seeking its own advantage over the other."

THE MOTHER OF HARLOTS

Revelation, Chapter 17, describes the Great Whore of Babylon, who represents false religion. Babylon's political and religious aspects bring down God's judgment. While political Babylon's judgment occurs just prior to the battle at Armageddon and results from the Antichrist's reign, religious Babylon's annihilation comes through the Antichrist and his federation of kings. The Antichrist abolishes religion, and persecutes its followers for not worshipping him alone. In Dwight Pentecost's Things To Come: A Study of Bible Eschatology, Pentecost quotes Scofield, who confirms: "Two 'Babylon's' are to be distinguished in the Revelation…Ecclesiastical Babylon is 'the great whore'(Rev. 17:1), and is destroyed by political Babylon (Rev. 17:15-18), that the beast may be the alone object of worship (II Thess. 2:3, 4; Rev. 13:15)."

As one reviews history, one realizes the identity of the woman in Revelation Chapter 17. She sits upon many waters, and is arrayed in purple and scarlet, and adorned with gold, precious stones, and pearls. Her hand holds a golden cup full of abominations and the filthiness of her fornication. Upon her head one sees words written in capital letters:

"MYSTERY, BABYLON THE GREAT, THE MOTHER OF HARLOTS AND ABOMINATIONS OF THE EARTH." Drunk with the blood of the saints (martyrs) she sits upon seven hills (Rev. 17:4-5, 9).

Harlotry, in the Bible, equals idolatry. When Israel worshipped other gods, God compared the nation to a harlot. The book of Hosea elaborates on this precept by its description of an adulterous wife and a faithful husband, symbolic of the unfaithfulness of Israel to God through idolatry. The bride of Christ is pure and holy, and she embraces truth. The harlot symbolizes all false teaching. She leads individuals away from the true God, to herself. The mother of harlots encompasses all doctrine, beliefs, practices, and ideology that diametrically opposes the truth of Jesus Christ.

Immorality, sorcery, and idolatry imprinted Babylonian society. The nation was famous throughout the ancient world for astronomy. They were astrologers first and foremost. Sorcerers and necromancers were more popular than physicians. Divination and the interpretation of dreams were common practice. Hepatoscopy, a favorite Babylonian method of divination, involved examining the livers of animals. Ezekiel confirms these Babylonian practices in declaring: "For the king of Babylon stands at the parting of the road, at the fork of the two roads, to use divination: he shakes the arrows, he consults the images, he looks at the liver" (Ezek.21:21). Heavily superstitious; the Babylonians were idolatrous, with innumerable gods. Historian Will Durant numbered their gods around 65,000.

The Babylonians worshipped one woman in particular. This woman is Ishtar, whom the Babylonians worshipped for being the mother of God. Her titles include "The Virgin," "The Holy Virgin," and "The Virgin Mother." Ishtar represented the divinity of bounteous motherhood. Those who worshiped her considered her a goddess of war as well as love. She stood over prostitutes as well as mothers. She called herself a caring courtesan. Babylonians represented Ishtar sometimes as a bearded bisexual deity, and sometimes as a nude female offering her breasts to suck. Though Babylonians referred to her as "The Virgin," this merely meant that her illicit lovers were free from all bonds of wedlock. Revelation 18:7 states: "She says in her heart, I sit as queen, and am no widow, and will not see sorrow." Ancient Babylonian prayers referred to her as "Queen of all cities, Queen of Heaven and Earth, Ishtar is great! Ishtar is Queen! My lady is exalted; my Lady is Queen." Revelation 17:16 names her "the whore." In later centuries, among Babylon's enemies, the upper classes called her the "whore of Babylon."

FALSE RELIGION

False religion led the Israelites from the true God to its teachings. Babylon's religious symbols and doctrines bore many similarities to those taught in the Scriptures, in part because the Jews lived within Babylonia and Jewish doctrine influenced their myths. Ancient Jews embraced the Babylonian religion, and God rebuked the Jews for following its practices. During Ahab's reign in Israel's northern kingdom, Jezebel, the Phoenician princess, instituted Baal worship and murdered the prophets of God. Baal was the Sun-god, the Life-Giving One, equivalent to Tammuz. Baal worship was part of Babylonian society, and caused the Babylonian invasion of Israel.

In Jeremiah 44:17-20, the Jews acknowledged to Jeremiah that they burned incense, and gave drink offerings to the Queen of Heaven. This passage mentions the "Queen of Heaven" four times. Four in the Bible represents the number of man, and man invented religion. From Babylon this mystery-religion spread to all the surrounding nations, and the symbols remained similar, including the image of the Queen of Heaven with a baby in her arms. Ashtoreth and Tammuz became Isis and Horus in Egypt, Aphrodite and Eros in Greece, Venus and Cupid in Italy, and bore many other names.

The Babylonian religion merged with Christianity during the reign of the Roman emperor Constantine. These combined beliefs became part of the Catholic Church. Historians Will and Ariel Durant recorded that, "Babylonian altars frequently sacrificed a lamb, as the substitute for man who gave it in exchange for his life… priests carried from sanctuary to sanctuary the image of Mardak, and performed the sacred drama of his death and resurrection. They anointed the idols with sweet-scented oils, burned incense before them, and clothed them with rich vestments."

The woman in Revelation 17 sits dressed as a harlot leading to herself the hearts of men. Revelation 17:2 tells us that the world's kings commit fornication with the Great Whore. The fornication committed is not merely physical, but spiritual adultery. As men deny the true Church of Jesus Christ by embracing the harlot's false teaching, they become corrupt in unholy union.

THE WHORE'S JUDGMENT

In the end times, the Great Whore sits upon the Beast-joined to his Kingdom-and later the Antichrist and his federation of kings destroy her. They carry her off, leaving her naked and burned. Her presence indicates political influence. Her destruction by the Beast reveals that she exercises limited power over the Antichrist and his federation of kings. Though present in the kingdom's early stages, she does not remain long after the entity becomes powerful. Her destruction occurs when the Antichrist claims to be god and demands worship of him alone. His ideology diametrically opposes her precepts. All religions threaten his imposed laws. Revelation 17 and Isaiah 47 describe the Great Whore's judgment by God. In verse 6, the Scriptures describe her as "drunk with the blood of the saints and with the blood of the martyrs." Verse 7 describes the Beast "carrying her." Initially the Bible pictures the woman sitting on the Beast-joined to his kingdom-which reveals that she has influence over the Beast. Later they carry her, indicating that she grows into a burden, and in verses 16 and 17 the Bible tells us: "And the ten horns which you saw on he beast, these will hate the harlot, make her desolate and naked, eat her flesh and burn her with fire."

The Whore's judgment comes from God. Making her desolate and naked, eating her flesh, and burning her with fire indicate that violence will be committed against her-such as spoiling the treasures of her churches, taking possession of her land, burning her Bibles, religious literature, statues, religious paraphernalia, and buildings, and persecuting her followers so that the Antichrist alone can be the sole object of worship. While she initially has influence over the Beast's kingdom, she does not remain long after his government becomes powerful. Her destruction occurs when the Antichrist claims to be a god and demands worship of him alone. All religions then become a threat to him, and he sets out to remove them from the face of the earth. In the past century many dictatorships arose and each of them eliminated freedom of religion and speech as the state and the dictator act as the objects of one's sole dedication. The Antichrist will limit these freedoms on a worldwide scale and the nations which do not willingly go along he will conquer.

Several Bible scholars teach that "the Whore" represents a one-world religion, which operates along with a one-world government. These writers cite the ecumenical movement that embraced many religions and supported left wing revolutionary groups as the forecasted one world religion. The movement endorsed liberation theology, which taught that Jesus was the first Marxist. Liberation theology used the Scripture to prove that the Bible provided the basis for Communism. The Catholic Church, one of the largest churches in the world, refused to join the Ecumenical Church.

Some expositors teach that the Antichrist heads the one world religion which launches the False Prophet. This author holds the view that the Whore of Babylon and the Beast operate separately and the Whore's location, religious teachings and influence over the area of the Beast intertwines them. Revelation 17:7 states that the beast "carries" the woman. The verse uses bastazo, the Greek word for carries which according to Strong's Lexicon means: 1) to take up with the hands, 2) to take up in order to carry or bear, to put upon one's self (something) to be carried, a) to bear what is burdensome, 3) to bear, to carry, a) to carry on one's person, b) to sustain, i.e. uphold, support, 4) to bear away, carry off. This woman clearly becomes a burden to these kings and the Scripture tells us "these shall hate the Whore." Verse 17 explains that they give their allegiance to the Beast who deifies himself and establishes his own religion (Dan. 11:39). The Revelation chapter specifies that the woman sits on the Beast because she shares the same location. Her teachings influence the leaders and people of the land.

4

FORGING A CATHOLIC EUROPE

The Bible depicts the Whore sitting on the Beast, signifying that she plays a principal role. Religion does play a part in European politics. Its precepts provided the ideology that prompted the European Union's formation. Religion has a voice in European politics through the Christian Democratic and Socialist political parties, which elect statesmen who share their beliefs. The leaders of these parties become the political representatives of their churches. During the French Revolution, as Democracy spread through Europe, so did Christian political parties. Most of these parties were Catholic. The Christian Democratic political movement would defend the Church's ultimate interests. This political party assumed responsibility for the social services that the Church was no longer in a position to provide. The Whore in part sits on the Beast through the Christian political parties that are responsible for the European Union's formation and evolution.

Catholic ideals influenced the European Union's founders. During World War II, French Foreign Minister Robert Schuman, German Chancellor Konrad Adenauer, and Alcide de Gasperi, each man exemplary

Catholics, had been hunted by Nazis and Fascists. De Gasperi-the founder of the Christian Democratic Party in Italy, and a militant Catholic activist and anti-fascist-became premier of Italy in 1945. He believed that the party man remained linked with his spiritual mother, the Church. His theological convictions influenced his public and private actions.

German Chancellor Konrad Adenaeur helped found the Christian Democratic Union (CDU) in Germany in 1945. He "typified a Catholic Germany in contrast to a pagan Germany." In 1949, the Frenchman Robert Schuman became France's foreign minister. He had wanted to become a priest, but gave the idea up to serve his faith in other ways. For him, politics was a priestly duty. All three men were politicians with high ideals. Pope Pius XII, who held strong political beliefs, sought to aid the cause of peace with the help of fellow Catholics. He and the leaders of the Christian Democratic parties formulated a plan. For the first time, leaders of the Catholic Church headed the French, Italian, and German governments. The Christian Democratic political parties aroused hopes of a new Christianity. The movement arranged religious gatherings where they planned political action. Vatican Europe became part of the political scene.

Europe, devastated by two world wars, directly felt the threat of two atheistic ideologies-communism and fascism. The European political leaders believed that the only way to have peace among nations would be if the nations aligned themselves in economic and political pursuits. Schuman proposed that France and Germany create a Coal and Steel Community, encompassing the two nation's production. Konrad Adenauer welcomed the idea as a way to prevent war among these two nations. They invited other nations to join as well. On May 9, 1950, the Schuman Declaration led to the first European Union and on April 18, 1951, European leaders signed the European Coal and Steel Community (ECSC) Treaty in Paris.

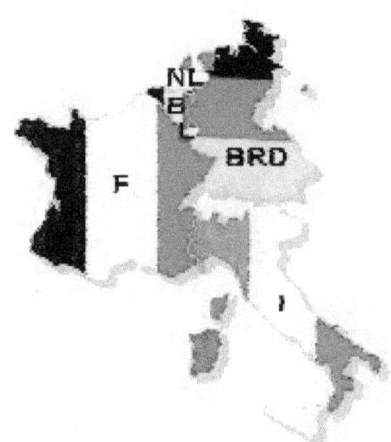

The entire Franco-German production of coal and steel resided under a higher authority. Its decisions bound France, Germany, and other member countries. A Council represented the interests of the Member States. The common assembly later became the Court of Justice. In their view, this foundation of a European federation was vital to the preservation of peace. The union would prevent war.

The French and German heavy industries urgently needed rebuilding. The ECSC would spur growth. This agreement marked the birth of the European Union. Ratified by the governments of France, the Federal Republic of Germany, Italy, Belgium, the Netherlands, and Luxembourg, the ECSC began functioning in 1952. It represented a revolutionary approach to international relations, as the first international organization with a federal governing body. This led to the drafting of the EURATOM (European Atomic Energy Community) and Common Market Treaties.

On March 25, 1957, European founders signed the EURATOM (European Atomic Energy Community) and the Common Market Treaties in Rome on one of its seven hills-Capitoline Hill.

Religion influenced the European Union's formation through political leaders who embraced its precepts. These men acted as key players in the Union's formation. They held the highest positions in its newly established organizations. Robert Schuman became the first president of the European Commission in 1958. Alcide de Gasperi held the presidential post of the ECSC Common Assembly in 1954. Monsignor Pierre Raffin, the Bishop of Metz, in Schuman's native Lorraine, launched a campaign for his beatification; the first step on the way to sainthood. Some Christian Democratic members of the European Parliament backed the initiative. Of Jacques Delors, the former EU Commission president, Stanley Hoffman, who writes on European Union affairs, wrote: "A former official of the French labor union inspired by progressive Catholic thought, he exemplifies the synthesis of Christian democracy and socialism on which the Community was built."

One's religious convictions greatly affect one's political beliefs. In the summer of 1998, the United Methodist News Service issued a press release stating that European churches were preparing to play a major role in the continued development of the European Union. The European Ecumenical Commission for Church and Society merged with the Conference of European Churches (CEC) into the Commission on Church and Society.

Members of this new commission included Methodists, Lutherans, Baptists, Anglicans, and the Orthodox. The Conference of European Churches comprised 123 different church bodies, and also cooperated with the Roman Catholic Church. Keith Clements, the conference's general secretary, commented: "For the first time in centuries, there's the possibility of creating a Europe without barriers, the challenge to the churches is whether they themselves can contribute to the unity."

Catholic thought provides the ideological basis for a united Europe, and presents itself as a political point of reference. The Church along with the unification of Europe, is simultaneously attempting to unify and strengthen itself. It aims to become the spiritual backbone of the evolving European Union. According to See Change, a publication for Catholic organizations, which reports on how the hierarchy of the Catholic Church involves itself in public policy debates: It seems that the bishops want the European Union to become an extension of the church, by confirming that European civilization, in the words of the pope, "emerged because the seed of Christianity was planted deep in Europe's soil." (Zenit, "Popes, proposals for European Charter of human rights, "September 24, 2000.)

Few democracies in Europe mention God in their constitutions but this did not deter the bishops from demanding that the European Union should do so. On January 13, 2003, Pope John Paul II gave his State of the World address to representatives of 177 countries in Vatican City. Concerning the European Union he stated: "The Holy See and all the Christian Churches have urged those drawing up the future Constitutional Treaty of the European Union to include a reference to Churches and religious institutions." He added: " A Europe which disavowed its past, which denied the fact of religion, and which had no spiritual dimension would be extremely impoverished in the face of the ambitious project which calls upon all its energies: constructing a Europe for all."

Within two weeks of the Pope's address, United Press International reported that the Pope was "lobbying European governments to officially recognize the European Union's Christian roots," and they reported on the Catholic Church's efforts to work a strong Christian reference into the preamble of the EU Constitution. The Vatican argues that "Christianity's fundamental role in shaping European culture should be acknowledged in what is destined to become the European Union's key document." Convention delegates are reluctant to involve religion in the new constitution; for fear that it might create additional problems for the Union. Dr. Ian Paisley of the Institute of Protestant Studies, whose web site promotes, defends, and maintains Bible Protestantism in Europe (http://www.ianpaisley.org/about.asp), exposes the papacy as the Beast of Revelation.

MEDIA INSIGHT (FATIMA.ORG)
EUROPEAN PARLIAMENT: THE MESSAGE OF FATIMA

Strasbourg, October 24, 2012 - On October 23, 2012 Father Nicholas Gruner of the Fatima Center in Canada and Catholic attorney and author Christopher A. Ferrara of the United States appeared at the headquarters of the EU in Strasbourg, France to speak in support of a motion for a declaration by the EU Parliament calling upon Pope Benedict XVI to carry out the Consecration of Russia to the Immaculate Heart of Mary.

The motion is being sponsored by two members of the Parliament of the European Union, the Honorable Mario Borghezio and the Honorable Lorenzo Fontana, who invited Father Gruner and Mr. Ferrara to speak in its support at the time of its official introduction. The motion refers to the threat of "great danger at the present time to world peace and the serenity of all European peoples" and notes that "the Blessed Virgin Mary has promised a long period of prosperity and peace, if and only if, the Holy Father will consecrate Russia in a solemn and public manner, as precisely specified by Her in the Message of Fatima."

The motion provides for a declaration by the EU Parliament formally requesting that "His Holiness, Pope Benedict XVI... fulfill the will of the Queen of Heaven" by performing the Consecration in order to address European and world problems. Speaking before the international press corps in the press hall of the EU Parliament headquarters in Strasbourg, Father Gruner and Mr. Ferrara made presentations in support of the measure, including a discussion of the content, undeniable authenticity, and absolute urgency of the Fatima Message for the Church and humanity at large. They were introduced by MPs, Borghezio and Fontana, who appeared with them at the press conference.

"This was a God-given opportunity to advance the cause of Our Lady of Fatima in a forum whose deliberations will have considerable impact at the Vatican. MEPs. Borghezio and Fontana are to be commended for their courageous defense of the Blessed Virgin before a hostile world. I pray the motion passes and the EU Parliament calls upon the Pope to do his duty," said Father Gruner. "I believe we succeeded in making a case for the Consecration of Russia that would appeal even to rational non-believers, who have nothing to lose by voting in favor this measure," said Mr. Ferrara.

The motion has been lodged with the EU Parliament as an official legislative document and will become part of the public record of EU proceedings. It has already attracted the signatures of a growing number of additional sponsors in the Parliament, including members from Italy, Austria and Ireland.

Revelation and offers some enlightening facts. His web site also exposes the Catholic Church's immorality and its political role within the European Union, and alerts its readers to EU legislation that infringes on the freedoms of European citizens. His article "The Vacant Seat Number 666 in the European Union Parliament," records:

"The prophetic significance of the European Union has been revealed as the saga unfolds. First, the sign which it chose as its symbol was the woman riding the Beast. This comes from a prophecy in Revelation 17. The depiction of the harlot woman was reproduced on the centenary stamp of the European Union, in a huge painting in the Parliament's new building in Brussels, and by a huge sculpture outside the new EU Council of Ministers Office in Brussels. The new European coinage, the euro, bears the same insignia. The Tower of Babel has been used on the posters emanating from Europe - a truly suggestive prophetic sign.Now, a massive Crystal Palace tower (officially called the Tower Building) houses the Fifth Parliament of Europe"

In November of 2008, the Catholic Church demanded that the EU enshrine Sunday observance into law. In October of 2009, the Catholic News Service reported Pope Benedict XVI asserting: "If European unity is based only on geography and economics, it cannot succeed in promoting the common good of all Europe's citizens and in helping the rest of the world. The recognition of the dignity of the human person and the obligation to work for the common good -- values Christianity fostered on the continent -- are what inspired the movement toward European unity and are the only guarantee of its success" The European Union did not bring those values to the 27 member countries, but rather it is these shared values that have given birth to and were like a gravitational force that drew the countries together and inspired them to form a union.

When the church recalls the Christian roots of Europe, it is not seeking a special status for itself, instead, it is calling Europeans to remember that the values that brought peace to the continent and freedom and dignity to its people must be allowed to continue nourishing it…Europe will not truly be herself if she cannot keep the originality that made her great. In the Pope's own words we see the image of the woman sitting on the Beast and her influence is clearly evident. So much so that contributors have devoted a page to Wikipedia, the online encyclopedia entitled "European Union- Holy See Relations," and another entry titled, "The European Union and the Catholic Church."

A few years back there was a web site dedicated to exposing the meaning of the EU flag. The site called itself "The EU Flag's True Symbolism Revealed." The writer presented the idea that the symbol derived from the Virgin Mary, and is a tribute to her. The EU's flag, a circle of twelve stars on a blue background, depicts Judeo-Christian symbolism. The twelve stars symbolize the twelve tribes of Israel, the twelve apostles, along with the twelve months in a year, and the Greek myth that speaks of the twelve labors Hercules performed to gain immortality.

The European Union bases many of its symbols on pagan myths; the very name Europe is from the Greek mythological Europa, a Phoenician noble woman kidnapped by Zeus who came to her as a bull and took her to the island of Crete where she became queen. Ian Paisley pointed out the similarity of Revelation Chapter 17 depiction of the harlot riding the beast and the EU's woman seated on the bull which are outside several of the European Union's institutions, as well as on the Greek euro coin.

Europa's name appeared on postage stamps commemorating the Council of Europe, issued in 1956. Furthermore, the dome of the European Parliament's Paul-Henri Spaak building contains a large mosaic by Aligi Sassu portraying the abduction of Europa with other elements of Greek mythology. Europa also serves as the national personification for Europe.

THE ROMAN LEGACY

If you live in Europe a gap of 2,000 years may seem to have put the Romans at a safe distance from your own lives and experience, but modern Europe with its Union is unthinkable without the Roman Empire. It is part of the story of how Europe came to be what it is today. The Romans are important as a conscious model, for good or ill, to successive generations. Why do they have such a powerful hold on Europe's development? A century ago, for those with imperialist ambitions, the Roman Empire represented a success story. Rome's story of conquest, at least in Europe and around the Mediterranean, was imitated, but never matched, by leaders from Charlemagne to Napoleon. The dream that one could not only conquer, but in so doing create a Pax Romana, a vast area of peace, prosperity and unity of ideas, was a genuine inspiration. And that genuine inspiration is what has preserved the legacy of Rome from the time of the Caesars up until the twenty first century.

5

BABYLONIAN EUROPE

God condemned all three aspects of Babylonian society-political, religious, and social. Besides being a hub for international trade, and religiously devoted to the Queen of Heaven, Babylonian society was immortal, steeped in superstition, divination, idolatry, and sexual promiscuity. The morals of Babylon shocked Alexander the Great, himself a drunkard. Temple prostitutes practiced sacred prostitution in Babylon until abolished by Constantine. Babylonians engaged in considerable premarital experience. Poor men prostituted their daughters for money. The indulgence in fleshly pleasures abounded.

Babylonian men acted effeminate. They wore their hair as long as the women did, dyed and curled it, perfumed their flesh, rouged their cheeks, and adorned themselves with necklaces, bangles, earrings, and pendants. This also describes many of today's rock groups, transvestites, transsexuals, and homosexual drag queens. In Europe today, materialism and superstition abound. Italian housewives practice forms of divination such as divining oil to read a migraine headache, or determining the sex of a baby by reading the movements of a needle over a pregnant woman's womb.

French society is one of the best educated in the world. Yet, in 1990, ten million French citizens consulted clairvoyants and astrologers. They spent three times as much on faith healers as they spent on family doctors. Almost half of the French population believes in faith healing. One in four believes in clairvoyants, and one in three believes in astrology. Many believe in the power of faith healers, astrologers, and palmists. In France, as many as sixty corporations use an organization called Divinitel, which employs astrology and tarot card reading for the recruitment of executives. In European society, extramarital affairs are so common that spouses expect each other to have lovers. Europeans view Americans' disdain for infidelity as being out of touch with the facts of life. Germany has legalized prostitution. Hard rock, punk, and new wave all originated in Europe, and their dress and music have influenced groups in the US and around the world.

The Green parties in Europe have revived a form of idolatry that originated with the Greeks: earth worship. To the Greeks, she was a goddess; earth as mother. Green policies for the preservation of the earth began in West Germany, spread through Europe and then into America. Ironically, the earth that these groups take such pains to preserve for future generations God will destroy. Mother Earth cannot save anyone from the coming Tribulation.

The book of Revelation foretells the destruction of Babylon. The Scriptures refer to Babylon as a "she." International trade characterizes her. God cites her as a deceiver of nations, and the means by which the merchants and great men of the earth trade (Revelation 18:7,23). The European Union's political ideology derives from the Whore's teachings. The act of uniting Europe to prevent war among its nations finds its roots in religious conviction. Nations will not wage war against one another while united in economic alliance. If nations align with one another they will eliminate war and achieve peace. The deception exists in the premise that worldwide democracy will ensure peace, justice, and human rights. Revelation 18:11-15 lists twenty-seven exported goods combined with categories of products. The 28th phrase lists "souls of men." Verse 23 concludes with: "For by thy sorceries were all the nations deceived."The Scriptures teach that man is sinful, and because of his nature there will be no peace on earth until the second coming of Jesus Christ.

During Nebuchadnezzar's reign, Jeremiah foretold Babylon's judgment in the latter days. Just as Nebuchadnezzar laid siege to Jerusalem and oppressed the Jews the Antichrist will do the same (Jeremiah 50:30). When the Antichrist treads down the nations, the nations become angry. Jeremiah 51:7 states: "Babylon was a golden cup in the Lord's hand that made all the earth drunk: The nations drank her wine; therefore the nations are deranged."

Revelation 17:4 tells us that abominations and filthiness of fornication fill the gold cup in her hand. The kings of the earth commit fornication with her and become drunk with the wine of her fornication. Revelation 18:3 adds that "the merchants of the earth have become rich through the abundance of her luxury." The rest of the chapter predicts her destruction. The remaining passages refer to her as the hub for trade for the earth's merchants. Upon her destruction, these merchants mourn, for they can no longer trade with her. After the Antichrist wreaks his havoc upon the earth, armies will go to fight against the European Union. Jeremiah 50:41 states:

"Behold, a people shall come from the North, and a great nation and many kings shall be raised up from the ends of the earth." "At the noise of the taking of Babylon the earth trembles, and the cry is heard among the nations" (Jeremiah 50:46).

God destroys political Babylon i.e. the final world empire. As Hitler was the spark for World War II, when he invaded and conquered nations in Europe; the Antichrist's swift and fast conquest will prompt powerful nations to wage war against him. Daniel 11:40 states that at the time of the end, the King of the South shall attack him: and the King of the North shall come against him like a whirlwind, with chariots, horsemen, and with many ships." When armies invade his land, the Antichrist enters into the attacking countries and defeats them. He conquers Egypt and North Africa. Hearing reports from the North and East, he goes forth with great fury to destroy. He ends up at a place prepared for him in Jerusalem (Daniel 11:42-45). Israel and the Middle East become part of Antichrist's conquered territory, according him the exact borders of the Roman Empire at the time of Christ. Jeremiah 4:6-7 tells us: "Set up the standard toward Zion: take refuge! Do not delay!: For I will bring disaster from the North, and great destruction. The lion has come up from his thicket, and the destroyer of the nations is on his way; he has gone forth from his place to make your land desolate; your cities will be laid waste without inhabitant."

The river Euphrates dries up, and prepares the way for the kings of the East. God draws the world's armies to the place called, in the Hebrew tongue, Armageddon (Rev. 16:12-16).

THE LEGACY OF POPE BENEDICT XVI

In 1990, a former Vatican-insider claimed that a titanic struggle was being waged to bring about a world political system. This contest, the now deceased Jesuit explained, was primarily between three players: international Leninism, transnational business elites, and the hand of the Vatican.

"Most of us are not competitors… We are the stakes. For the competition is about who will establish the first one-world system of government… No one can be exempted from its effects. No sector of our lives will remain untouched."

Almost twenty years have passed since Malachi Martin drew attention to this three-way quest. At the time his assertions seemed over-the-top. Granted, the idea of a world government via communism wasn't new as decades of Cold War posturing still played in our minds. And the writing was on the wall in respect to the growing power of international corporate and financial elites. The Roman Catholic Church has always seen itself as the successor to the Roman Empire. Its ambitions are imperial as well as spiritual. It laid the foundations of Western civilization in Europe. It also sees itself as the spiritual leader of the European Union in which several treaties have been signed by the European Union in Rome which houses Vatican City.

Pope Benedict XVI during his reign as head of the Roman Catholic Church had worked quickly to restore the Church as the spiritual force that would unite Europe, the way it did in the time of Charlemagne. He appealed both to traditionalists (e.g., by restoring the Tridentine mass) and to secularists (e.g., by his recent concession with respect to condoms). He has underlined (in his speech at Regensburg) the contrast of Catholicism and Islam, and made room for disaffected Anglicans to join the Catholic Church. He was establishing new ecumenical ties to the Lutheran and Eastern churches.

Despite the recent scandals affecting the Church, Benedict was on the offensive. A German himself, he was working to forge a united Europe, led by Germany, with the Catholic Church as its spiritual head. The Vatican also several years ago issued a little known booklet for their private eyes only called 'Project Vatican.' 34 The internal document is a blueprint for the "restoration of the global kingdom of Jesus Christ in the third millennium." Contained within the booklet is also the Vatican's plan for the domination of America, listing their goals and true evil purposes. Although the booklet was initially kept hidden from the public parts of it have leaked on the internet.

The Vatican blueprint of world domination has a five-prong approach, including: The Jesuit infiltration of the English colonies on the North American continent (Phase 1)

- Jesuit control of Christian schools and universities (Phase 2)
- Roman Catholic Control exercised through Vatican operatives in the United States military, judiciary and media (Phase 3)
- The weakening of the U.S. military, both in strength and resolve, in preparation for the Vatican-led
- One World Government (Phase 4)
- Total control of all institutions and resources on earth, including political, military, economic, educational systems for the purpose of ensuring global peace, prosperity and order (Phase 5)

The Vatican writers' introduction to Project Vatican states:

"Phase 1 through Phase IV have taken 523 years to complete and at the dawn of the third millennium is poised to launch Phase V. This will necessitate cooperation of the citizens of every nation on the planet on a massive scale and in previously untested numbers,"

The writers of the 18 page booklet dedicated their efforts to Phase V, saying strategies have been in full effect albeit for varying lengths of time. Further, they claimed the execution of their first strategy of Phase V began more than 150 years ago, the strategy being listed as, "Devotion to the Sacred Heart of Jesus and to the Immaculate Heart of Mary through the perpetuation of visions, miracles and revelations."

Other strategies under the Vatican's Phase V for world domination include: Dilution of the eschatological models of Biblical prophecy.

- The alignment of the homosexual agenda with religious and racial equality, guaranteeing a support base sufficient in number to Biblical Christian fundamentalism into the category of "hate speech."

In the core section of this point, Vatican writers reveal how they plan to obtain loyalty to the Pope, saying, "The Protestants' lack of a governing authority has resulted in a sheep-like obedience to civil governments. Such social compliance, coupled with capitalistic greed has made Christian fundamentalists extremely vulnerable to social engineering."

The last section tells Vatican loyalists what they can do in order to speed-up Rome's plans, adding, "Attend non-Catholic churches that are not yet RCEA affiliates for the purpose of encouraging their ministries to join the RCEA. Make audio recordings of their responses and deliver these recordings to your RCEA representative. Report all statements by non-Catholics of a racially-biased, homophobic or anti Catholic nature to your RCEA representative." For many, the belief that the Holy See was pursuing a vision of world government was simply too much. After all, this ancient hub of Roman Catholicism had a reputation - especially among Europe's agnostic youth - as an institution of old men, steeped in tradition, procession and ceremony. Never mind that the history of the Continent, more often than not, revolved around the Vatican's political prowess.

In the summer of 2009, the Holy See's political cards were revealed in a major papal document. Harkening back to Malachi Martin's talk of world government, the most powerful religious office on the planet had promoted a world political authority to manage the global economy. Food security, disarmament, and peace would follow suit.

When the Pope agrees with Mikhail Gorbachev, the Secretary-General of the United Nations, Henry Kissinger, the President of the European Union, and other secular leaders on the need for global governance and a new world order, we can know that the world has indeed experienced a "harmonic convergence" and entered a new age. With the publication of Caritas in Veritate, the encyclical on Catholic social teaching released in July 2009 by Benedict XVI, this dark convergence happened.

Pope Urges New World Economic Order

By RACHEL DONADIO
Published July 7, 2009

VATICAN CITY — Pope Benedict XVI on Tuesday called for a radical rethinking of the global economy, criticizing a growing divide between rich and poor and urging the establishment of a "world political authority" to oversee the economy and work for the "common good."

In addition, new movements - carefully tended by some of the best-connected people on the planet - are mobilizing people at the grass-roots level for a new degree of religious unity. The United Religions Initiative, a fast-growing interfaith organization first announced in 1995 in San Francisco, is an example established now, in plain sight. The only open issues are who will direct this new planetary regime, for which goals, and at what cost to Western liberty and Christian faith.

Angela Merkel, the Chancellor of Germany, agreed on the need for "more global order," "no matter what it costs." In a speech given on the 20th anniversary of the fall of the Berlin Wall, she said, "This world will not be a peaceful one if we do not work for more global order and more multilateral cooperation."

When discussing the December 2009 UN climate summit meeting in Copenhagen, Merkel said that nations must be ready to put "the greater good" above their "narrow interests;" she asked, "Are the nation states ready and willing to give competencies over to multilateral organizations, no matter what it costs?"

Herman Van Rompuy, the President of the Council of the European Union, is a conservative Catholic. Nevertheless, he too is enthusiastic for "the global management of our planet." In November 2009, when accepting his new post, Van Rompuy said, "We are living through exceptionally difficult times: the financial crisis and its dramatic impact on employment and budgets, the climate crisis which threatens our very survival. ... Yet these problems can be overcome by common efforts in and between our countries. 2009 is also the first year of global governance, with the establishment of the G20 in the middle of the financial crisis. The climate conference in Copenhagen is another step towards the global management of our planet. Our mission is one of hope, supported by acts and action."

In the past, the proponents of "global governance" have faced Papal skepticism or opposition. With the publication of Caritas in Veritate, Benedict XVI had himself come out strongly for a new world order. He might have wished to put a new international system to different uses than those supported by Gorbachev, Merkel, Kissinger, or others - but he agreed that a new international system, "a true world political authority," must come into being. Based on his writings in the 1980s and 1990s, Ratzinger had built a reputation as an opponent of utopianism and of any plans to build a new world order. However, with Caritas in Veritate, he had now revealed his own sweeping plan for "global governance." Evidence of this is not limited to the much- discussed paragraph of Caritas in Veritate that calls for creating a "true world political authority," it is present throughout the whole document.

6

POLITICAL POWER: THE BASIS OF THE NEW ORDER

Benedict's new "world political authority" would have power, backed by force, over the key sectors of the global economy. Throughout the long, densely written pontifical document, the same theme emerges repeatedly. He said:

"Political authority also involves a wide range of values, which must not be overlooked in the process of constructing a new order of economic productivity, socially responsible and human in scale."

Benedict thought that "political authority" could be used safely and effectively for "constructing a new order of economic productivity." However, post-1789 history is littered with the corpses of those slain in human efforts to construct a "new order" of any kind, however beneficent the original intent may have been. As a result of the world economic crisis, Benedict expected (and approved) growth of State power, at the national and international level: "The integrated economy of the present day does not make the role of States redundant, but rather it commits governments to greater collaboration with one another. Both wisdom and prudence suggest not being too precipitous in declaring the demise of the State. In terms of the resolution of the current crisis, the State's role seems destined to grow, as it regains many of its competences. In some nations, moreover, the construction or reconstruction of the State remains a key factor in their development."

His prediction that the current slump will increase government power has already been proven correct - but it is also clear that Benedict approved of this development. Benedict said, "Alongside economic aid, there needs to be aid directed towards reinforcing the guarantees proper to the State of law: a system of public order and effective imprisonment that respects human rights, truly democratic institutions."

Note well: for Benedict, one of the two elements defining the rule of law is "a system of public order and effective imprisonment." "Respect for human rights" is a very elastic constraint on a prison system and on a government; most governments claim that they do this. For Benedict, prison is integral to the New State that he has proposed. (Nor is Benedict's inquisitorial definition of the "State of law" an artifact of a bad English translation; in the Latin version of the encyclical, the same sentence reads "Praeter auxilia oeconomica adesse debent subsidia, quae proprias cautiones Status iuris roborent, systema nempe ordinis publici et efficientis carcerationis, hominum iuribus servatis, quae ad instituta vere democratica spectant."

Benedict proposed to ride the wave of globalization, using its power as a way to carry out "unprecedented ... large-scale redistribution of wealth on a world-wide scale." He said, "'globalization, a priori, is neither good nor bad. It will be what people make of it.' We should not be its victims, but rather its protagonists, acting in the light of reason, guided by charity and truth. Blind opposition would be a mistaken and prejudiced attitude, incapable of recognizing the positive aspects of the process, with the consequent risk of missing the chance to take advantage of its many opportunities for development. The processes of globalization, suitably understood and directed, open up the unprecedented possibility of large-scale redistribution of wealth on a world-wide scale ... The transition inherent in the process of globalization presents great difficulties and dangers that can only be overcome if we are able to appropriate the underlying anthropological and ethical spirit that drives globalization towards the humanizing goal of solidarity. Unfortunately this spirit is often overwhelmed or suppressed by ethical and cultural considerations of an individualistic and utilitarian nature. Globalization is a multifaceted and complex phenomenon which must be grasped in the diversity and unity of all its different dimensions, including the theological dimension. In this way it will be possible to experience and to steer the globalization of humanity in relational terms, in terms of communion and the sharing of goods."

Benedict called his readers to be "protagonists" - leading players and advocates - of globalization. As is usual for collectivists and utopians, Benedict scorned the "individualistic and utilitarian" opposition to a new economic order. He dismissed resistance to globalization as "blind," seeming to ignore clear-sighted opponents of this trend. His hope for "unprecedented... large-scale redistribution of wealth on a world- wide scale" should raise alarms for anyone who is familiar with the history of post-1789 radicalism of the left or of the right.

Large-scale, rapid wealth redistribution has always been accompanied by dictatorship, famine, and violence; there is no reason to expect that the results would be different under any conceivable future globalist regime. If Benedict has discerned an "underlying anthropological and ethical spirit that drives globalization towards the humanizing goal of solidarity," it makes sense to question his discernment in this (and related) matters.

Benedict explicitly called for redistribution of world energy resources to poor nations. In addition to energy-saving technical change and lower energy consumption by consumers and businesses in developed nations, he said,

"What is also needed, though, is a worldwide redistribution of energy resources, so that countries lacking those resources can have access to them. The fate of those countries cannot be left in the hands of whoever is first to claim the spoils, or whoever is able to prevail over the rest."

Benedict repeated this call for redistribution of energy resources in his message for the 2010 Day of Peace. This might sound reasonable at first, and it is true that energy-poor underdeveloped nations need such assistance. However, there are insurmountable practical questions, especially given the fallen human nature of anyone who will manage such redistribution. Who will take what from whom, under what law, and by what regulatory standard, to give to whom, and with what means of enforcement? Those who would carry out this redistribution will be no wiser, no more peace-loving, no more just, and no more honest than the current crop of world political leaders, bureaucrats, and police. Benedict emphasized the necessity for the Church to be active in the political world. He said, "The Church has a responsibility towards creation and she must assert this responsibility in the public sphere."

(In his message for the 2010 World Day of Peace, Benedict said the same.) In his encyclical, Benedict said, "The Christian religion and other religions can offer their contribution to development only if God has a place in the public realm, specifically in regard to its cultural, social, economic, and particularly its political dimensions. The Church's social doctrine came into being in order to claim 'citizenship status' for the Christian religion." However, to say that "the Christian religion" can offer its "contribution to development only if God has a place in the public realm ... particularly its political dimensions" casts disrespect on the ministry of Jesus, who said that "my kingship is not of this world" (John 18:36). It also ignores the pre-Constantine Church, which - despite centuries of persecution - managed to overturn the religious order of the world's greatest empire without wielding any State power whatsoever.

As the capstone of his analysis, Benedict proposed the erection of a "true world political authority" with "real teeth" and wielding sufficient power to manage economics, food, armaments, environmental protection, and migration for the whole world: "In the face of the unrelenting growth of global interdependence, there is a strongly felt need, even in the midst of a global recession, for a reform of the United Nations Organization, and likewise of economic institutions and international finance, so that the concept of the family of nations can acquire real teeth." This new regime would have wide responsibilities: "implementing the principle of the responsibility to protect," to "give direction to international cooperation for the development of all peoples in solidarity. To manage the global economy ... to bring about integral and timely disarmament, food security and peace; to guarantee the protection of the environment and to regulate migration: for all this, there is urgent need of a true world political authority." A global authority with enough power to manage all these "portfolios" would necessarily be despotic.

Benedict imagined that the "world authority" he seeks could be directed by "the values of charity in truth," so as to create a new "social order that at last conforms to the moral order." This authority would be "universally recognized" and would have "the effective power" to carry out its vast mandate. He said, "Such an authority would need to be regulated by law, to observe consistently the principles of subsidiarity and solidarity, to seek to establish the common good, and to make a commitment to securing authentic integral human development inspired by the values of charity in truth. Furthermore, such an authority would need to be universally recognized and to be vested with the effective power to ensure security for all, regard for justice, and respect for rights. Obviously it would have to have the authority to ensure compliance with its decisions from all parties, and also with the coordinated measures adopted in various international forums. ... The integral development of peoples and international cooperation require the establishment of a greater degree of international ordering, marked by subsidiarity, for the management of globalization. They also require the construction of a social order that at last conforms to the moral order, to the interconnection between moral and social spheres." Understanding the basis of

Benedict's manifesto, only an ecclesiastical propagandist could deny that Benedict was seeking a powerful world government.

MEDIA ROLE: "ENGINEERING CHANGES IN ATTITUDE"

With a new world order would come the need to propagandize the people. Benedict had this in view, since he assumed that a key role of the mass media is "engineering changes in attitude towards reality and the human person" for their audience. He said, "Given the media's fundamental importance in engineering changes in attitude towards reality and the human person, we must reflect carefully on their influence, especially in regard to the ethical-cultural dimension of globalization and the development of peoples in solidarity. ... This means that they can have a civilizing effect not only when, thanks to technological development, they increase the possibilities of communicating information, but above all when they are geared towards a vision of the person and the common good that reflects truly universal values. ... To achieve goals of this kind, they need to focus on promoting the dignity of persons and peoples, they need to be clearly inspired by charity and placed at the service of truth, of the good, and of natural and supernatural fraternity."

The same questions need to be asked here that would be asked of any other would-be social planner who wishes to manage us "for our own good": who will define the goals that the media are to promote; who will enforce these rules, and by what means? What room will there be for dissenting views? As with all utopias, the question is: who is to engineer whom, and for whose benefit? The notion that writers (or others in the media) should be engineers of their audience is totalitarian in origin and intent. As Stalin told a meeting of writers in October 1932, "You are engineers of human souls."

Dreaming of a new order in the current age, based on "adhering to the values of Christianity" Benedict has proposed "building a good society" and "integral human development" based on worldwide adherence to "the values of Christianity," as defined by the Church. Early in the encyclical, Benedict said, "practicing charity in truth helps people to understand that adhering to the values of Christianity is not merely useful but essential for building a good society and for true integral human development. ... Without truth, charity is confined to a narrow field devoid of relations. It is excluded from the plans and processes of promoting human development of universal range, in dialogue between knowledge and praxis."

He has offered his own vision of total social reform, based on "plans and processes" to promote "human development of universal range." Until now, preparing plans to direct all aspects of human development has been a hallmark of utopians and socialists. Now, Benedict is - for his own reasons - singing along with that choir. Benedict was inclined to view globalization, in its essence, as good: "The truth of globalization as a process and its fundamental ethical criterion are given by the unity of the human family and its development towards what is good."

He said that globalization "has been the principal driving force behind the emergence from underdevelopment of whole regions, and in itself it represents a great opportunity. Nevertheless, without the guidance of charity in truth, this global force could cause unprecedented damage and create new divisions within the human family. Hence charity and truth confront us with an altogether new and creative challenge, one that is certainly vast and complex. It is about broadening the scope of reason and making it capable of knowing and directing these powerful new forces, animating them within the perspective of that 'civilization of love' whose seed God has planted in every people, in every culture." Benedict imagined that somehow, those who exercise "charity in truth" while "adhering to the values of Christianity" will be able to direct globalization in order to build a "civilization of love."

In this vision, Christian leadership, after "broadening the scope of reason and making it capable of knowing and directing these powerful new forces" (a formulation that could have come from the French Revolution), will be able to govern globalization - a political and economic force that has thus far proven able to evade restraints from nations and from today's international organizations. Also, given the anti- Christian and anti-traditional track record of the UN and the European Union, and given the current balance of forces in the world (in which Communists, secularists, Muslims, Hindus, and followers of other faiths outweigh traditional Christians of all denominations together), it is not clear how it will ever be possible to build a "civilization of love" based on "adhering to the values of Christianity." Does Benedict imagine that somehow, before the Return of Christ, the whole world will accept Christianity - and governance on Christian norms?

"In all cultures there are examples of ethical convergence, some isolated, some interrelated, as an expression of the one human nature, willed by the Creator; the tradition of ethical wisdom knows this as the natural law. This universal moral law provides a sound basis for all cultural, religious and political dialogue, and it ensures that the multi-faceted pluralism of cultural diversity does not detach itself from the common quest for truth, goodness and God. Thus adherence to the law etched on human hearts is the precondition for all constructive social cooperation. ... The Christian faith, by becoming incarnate in cultures and at the same time transcending them, can help them grow in universal brotherhood and solidarity, for the advancement of global and community development."

However, not all cultures accept the existence of natural law; those who acknowledge it do not necessarily agree on its principles. It is utopian to imagine that such fundamental disagreement on the nature of reality and the source of morality will be peacefully overcome in the foreseeable future. Benedict placed "charitable" political action on a par with individual charity: "The more we strive to secure a common good corresponding to the real needs of our neighbors, the more effectively we love them. Every Christian is called to practice this charity, in a manner corresponding to his vocation and according to the degree of influence he wields in the polis. This is the institutional path - we might also call it the political path - of charity, no less excellent and effective than the kind of charity which encounters the neighbor directly, outside the institutional mediation of the polis."

To ensure that no one missed his message, he made it clear in the conclusion of the encyclical that he was addressing those who work "alongside 'political authorities and those working in the field of economics": "God's love calls us to move beyond the limited and the ephemeral, it gives us the courage to continue seeking and working for the benefit of all, even if this cannot be achieved immediately and if what we are able to achieve, alongside political authorities and those working in the field of economics, is always less than we might wish." When Benedict said that "the political path" is "no less excellent and effective than the kind of charity which encounters the neighbor directly," he made it seem that Christ, St. Francis of Assisi, St. John Bosco, and Blessed Teresa of Calcutta all missed their targets in directing their charity to their neighbors, rather than agitating for political reform.

Benedict said, "Man's earthly activity, when inspired and sustained by charity, contributes to the building of the universal city of God, which is the goal of the history of the human family. In an increasingly globalized society, the common good and the effort to obtain it cannot fail to assume the dimensions of the whole human family, that is to say, the community of peoples and nations, in such a way as to shape the earthly city in unity and peace, rendering it to some degree an anticipation and a prefiguration of the undivided city of God." If the "earthly city" prefigures the "city of God," and the unified "earthly city" is to cover "the whole human family," there would be no reason not to build a new world system that would be like "a tower with its top in the heavens" (Genesis 11:4). From Genesis through Daniel to Revelation, Scripture warns against such human hubris. Several other unusual theological ideas make their appearance in this encyclical:

THE NECESSITY OF USING REASON TO PURIFY FAITH?

Benedict said that "Reason always stands in need of being purified by faith: this also holds true for political reason, which must not consider itself omnipotent. For its part, religion always needs to be purified by reason in order to show its authentically human face." Later in the encyclical, he said that in the face of ethical challenges posed by biotechnology, "reason and faith can come to each other's assistance. Only together will they save man. Entranced by an exclusive reliance on technology, reason without faith is doomed to flounder in an illusion of its own omnipotence. Faith without reason risks being cut off from everyday life."

It is true that without a living faith in the one true God, application of human reason to politics is likely to produce disaster; in that sense, reason does indeed need to be "'purified by faith." However, it is strange for any Christian to claim that "religion" must always be "'purified by reason." This may be true for man-created religions, or for man- made reconstructions of Christianity. But Christian faith is not one of many man-made or partially true "religions;" it is (or should be) a relationship with Christ, who is uniquely the human face of God. How could that faith (and such a relationship between God and man) need purification by reason?

The Scriptures do not present Christian faith as something to be deduced or purified by human reason; St. Paul testifies that Christ is folly (not reason) to the Greeks, of that era or of this one: "Has not God made foolish the wisdom of the world? ... For Jews demand signs and Greeks seek wisdom, but we preach Christ crucified, a stumbling block to Jews and folly to Gentiles." (1 Corinthians 1:20-23) In any event, it is not true that "reason and faith" together can "save man;" the only Savior is Christ. How could any Christian - let alone the current occupant of the Chair of Peter - suggest otherwise?

FIDELITY TO MAN?

Benedict put "fidelity to man" rather than to God at the center of his social vision, and seemed to view truth as something that is assembled into "a unity" by the Church from "fragments" found in "whichever branch of knowledge":

"Fidelity to man requires fidelity to the truth, which alone is the guarantee of freedom ... and of the possibility of integral human development. For this reason the Church searches for truth, proclaims it tirelessly and recognizes it wherever it is manifested. This mission of truth is something that the Church can never renounce. Her social doctrine is a particular dimension of this proclamation: it is a service to the truth which sets us free. Open to the truth, from whichever branch of knowledge it comes, the Church's social doctrine receives it, assembles into a unity the fragments in which it is often found, and mediates it within the constantly changing life-patterns of the society of peoples and nations."

This vision of truth is depersonalized, and is a far cry from the clear testimony of Christ, who told His followers that He is "the way, the truth, and the life" (John 14:6). A truth that is assembled by human reason its place in a university seminar, but it will not be the same saving truth as "the faith which was once for all delivered to the saints" (Jude 3). At the beginning of this same paragraph, Benedict said that "The Church does not have technical solutions to offer and does not claim 'to interfere in any way in the politics of States." It seems inconsistent for him then to propose that the Church assemble a unified social truth from fragments offered by the world's branches of knowledge, and then offer this new construct to the "society of peoples and nations." A strange faith in man also appeared when Benedict warned against "rejection, not only of the distorted and unjust way in which progress is sometimes directed, but also of scientific discoveries themselves, which, if well used, could serve as an opportunity of growth for all. The idea of a world without development indicates a lack of trust in man and in God. It is therefore a serious mistake to undervalue human capacity to exercise control over the deviations of development or to overlook the fact that man is constitutionally oriented towards 'being more.'"

Benedict's justified rejection of back-to-nature primitivism comes with a condemnation of an odd pairing, "lack of trust in man and in God." But nowhere in Scripture are we called to exercise "trust in man," let alone to trust man in the way that we are to trust God. Instead, we are told to have faith in God, and to "put not your trust in princes" (Psalm 146:3). Benedict called on mankind to manage technical progress by using "human capacity to exercise control over the deviations of development," even though the ongoing pollution of land, air, and water shows how well we exercise this "human capacity" in practice. If Benedict sought to solve environmental crises by establishing new laws and bureaucracies to "exercise control over the deviations of development," he (and we) face the intractable reality of fallen human nature. No army of saints and angels is available to make and enforce such new controls; the only available people are people.

Benedict also overlooks the ambiguity in "the fact that man is constitutionally oriented towards 'being more.'" We are fallen; the line between good and evil is now drawn through each human heart. Our better part seeks "being more" by following God; our evil part seeks to "be more" for ourselves against God, ever again eating illicitly of the Tree of the Knowledge of Good and Evil, and ever again building new Towers of Babel.

THE WORK OF THE CHURCH: "INTEGRAL HUMAN DEVELOPMENT"?

Benedict offered his readers two truths: "The first is that the whole Church, in all her being and acting - when she proclaims, when she celebrates, when she performs works of charity - is engaged in promoting integral human development. She has a public role over and above her charitable and educational activities: all the energy she brings to the advancement of humanity and of universal fraternity is manifested when she is able to operate in a climate of freedom. In not a few cases, that freedom is impeded by prohibitions and persecutions, or it is limited when the Church's public presence is reduced to her charitable activities alone.

The second truth is that authentic human development concerns the whole of the person in every single dimension." There are several oddities here. Benedict said that the aim of the Church "in all her being and acting" - including teaching and worship ("when she proclaims, when she celebrates") - is "promoting integral human development." This is a new doctrine, quite different from Christ's post-Resurrection mandate that the Church is to "make disciples of all nations, baptizing them in the name of the Father and of the Son and of the Holy Spirit, teaching them to observe all that I have commanded you" (Matthew 28:19-20). The earthly goals that Benedict stated ("advancement of humanity and of universal fraternity") are good in themselves, as far as they go, but they are effects of the Church and her members acting in accord with God's will. "Seek first his kingdom and his righteousness, and all these things will be yours as well" (Matthew 6:33). When Benedict says that "authentic human development concerns the whole of the person in every single dimension," he is fostering an ideology that would govern every aspect of human life: a utopian vision in religious garb.

BENEDICT'S "NEW HUMANISTIC SYNTHESIS"

Like other utopians - and like Gorbachev, Kissinger, and other leaders who support a new world order - Benedict saw the post-2007 world crisis as an opportune occasion for radical change, a "new humanistic synthesis" and a "new vision for the future" that will affect "nothing less than the destiny of man." He said that "the current crisis ... presents us with choices that cannot be postponed concerning nothing less than the destiny of man, who, moreover, cannot rescind from his nature. ... The different aspects of the crisis, its solutions, and any new development that the future may bring, are increasingly interconnected, they imply one another, they require new efforts of holistic understanding and a new humanistic synthesis. ... The current crisis obliges us to re plan our journey, to set ourselves new rules and to discover new forms of commitment, to build on positive experiences and to reject negative ones. The crisis thus becomes an opportunity for discernment, in which to shape a new vision for the future." Later in the encyclical, Benedict added, "The significant new elements in the picture of the development of peoples today in many cases demand new solutions. These need to be found together, respecting the laws proper to each element and in the light of an integral vision of man ... Remarkable convergences and possible solutions will then come to light."

When Benedict saw the world crisis as "an opportunity for discernment, in which to shape a new vision for the future," he was following the logic of American political leaders. In November 2008, Rahm Emanuel, President Obama's chief of staff, told a Wall Street Journal conference of chief executives, "You never want a serious crisis to go to waste. ... Things that we had postponed for too long, that were long-term, are now immediate and must be dealt with. This crisis provides the opportunity for us to do things that you could not do before."

BENEDICT'S CALL FOR "SUBSIDIARITY": A DEFENSE AGAINST GLOBALIST TYRANNY?

Benedict called for "a dispersed political authority, effective on different levels ... The articulation of political authority at the local, national and international levels is one of the best ways of giving direction to the process of economic globalization. It is also the way to ensure that it does not actually undermine the foundations of democracy," indicating that he did not wish to build a fully centralized global regime. Later in the encyclical, Benedict restated his call for decentralization of political power in the context of global governance.

"Subsidiarity is first and foremost a form of assistance to the human person via the autonomy of intermediate bodies. ... Hence the principle of subsidiarity is particularly well-suited to managing globalization and directing it towards authentic human development. In order not to produce a dangerous universal power of a tyrannical nature, the governance of globalization must be marked by subsidiarity, articulated into several layers and involving different levels that can work together. Globalization certainly requires authority, insofar as it poses the problem of a global common good that needs to be pursued. This authority, however, must be organized in a subsidiary and stratified way, if it is not to infringe upon freedom and if it is to yield effective results in practice."

This nod in the direction of decentralized authority has given great reassurance to many American conservative commentators in the encyclical. It makes it seem as if Benedict has signed off on the equivalent of the Tenth Amendment to the US Constitution: "The powers not delegated to the United States by the Constitution, nor prohibited by it to the States, are reserved to the States respectively, or to the people." However, there is little basis for such reassurance. Benedict himself places an important restriction on the scope of subsidiarity and decentralization in the next paragraph of the encyclical. He says, "The principle of subsidiarity must remain closely linked to the principle of solidarity and vice versa, since the former without the latter gives way to social privatism, while the latter without the former gives way to paternalist social assistance that is demeaning to those in need."

This is the same logic that supporters of ever-stronger Federal authority have used since World War I to justify their own centralization of power in the US. There is no realistic reason to believe that the new rulers of a world government will show any more respect for localism and the virtues of decentralization than the US government has done with respect to states, counties, and cities. In his April 18, 2008 address to the UN General Assembly, Benedict said, "The United Nations embodies the aspiration for a 'greater degree of international ordering' ... inspired and governed by the principle of subsidiarity, and therefore capable of responding to the demands of the human family through binding international rules and through structures capable of harmonizing the day-to-day unfolding of the lives of peoples. This is all the more necessary at a time when ... the world's problems call for interventions in the form of collective action by the international community."

Benedict thus accepted the UN as an example of an authoritative world body "governed by the principle of subsidiarity" and able to establish "binding international rules" that will harmonize "the day-to-day unfolding of the lives of peoples." In other words, the "world political authority" envisioned by Benedict would - by design - reach out and touch all of us in our daily lives. Furthermore, the concept of "subsidiarity" is built into the treaties that govern the European Union; anyone can see how well that is working to defend national sovereignty, traditional values, and Christian faith in Europe. If the bureaucratic, corrupt, arrogant, tyrant-coddling, pro-socialist, population- controlling United Nations and European Union are examples of the "subsidiarity" that Benedict would rely upon to curb despotism by the "world political authority" that he favors, then we should all re-read Orwell's 1984 and Solzhenitsyn's Gulag Archipelago for tips on how to survive in the new world order.

THE CHURCH IGNITES POLITICAL GLOBALISM

Caritas in Veritate should be seen as what it is: a theological and political earthquake. The Roman Catholic Church, which was once a guardian of tradition worldwide, now wishes to use radical means (a "true world political authority") for its own ends. It is as if Benedict had wished to mount and ride a wild beast, and imagined that he (and those who believe as he does) would be able to direct that fierce beast's course. Ordinary prudence - even without reference to the dire symbolism of Revelation 17:3-18 - should have warned the Vatican against such folly. Europeans have already tried using radical means to support conservative goals; the results of that 20th century experiment in Italy, Portugal, Germany, Spain, and Vichy France are written in letters of blood and fire. Seeking a world government that is governed and limited by natural law and Christian tradition is akin to seeking dry water or square circles. Lord Acton, a Catholic historian in 19th Century England, made a warning that the Vatican ought to have heeded.

"Power tends to corrupt and absolute power corrupts absolutely. Great men are almost always bad men, even when they exercise influence and not authority: still more when you super add the tendency or the certainty of corruption by authority."

No power could be more absolute than that of "world ruler," and such is the post which (despite the fig-leaf invocation of "subsidiarity") Benedict proposes to create. Even the billionaire leftist utopian George Soros recognized that full-scale global government would be a threat to freedom. In August 2006, he said, "I'm against global government. Now [laughing] if you don't like a national government, you can move someplace else. A global government would probably interfere with our freedom more than national governments." Several months later, Soros added, "A global government could not avoid being repressive even if it were built on liberal principles. A global open society could not even be as closely integrated as the European Union because the affinity among the member states would be less pronounced." Essentially, an avowedly globalist "change agent" has a more sober perspective on global government than the Pope. In September 2009, a columnist for the London Telegraph provided a realistic view of global governance:

"The idea of global governance is meaningless without mechanisms to enforce it, so what are we talking about here? World government? A system of laws and policing which would be beyond the reach of the electorates of individual countries, and therefore have no direct democratic accountability to the peoples of those nations? Even assuming that such institutions did not take on a self-justifying life of their own - which history teaches us is almost inevitable - and that they remained fastidiously responsive to the heads of national governments, they would still be, by definition, supranational. In other words, their function would be precisely to ignore those needs and interests of individual countries which might endanger the welfare of the larger entity. And the welfare of that larger entity would be judged by - what? ... It is hard enough for a leader to remain in touch with the consciousness of his own people: playing to a global electorate puts almost any politician out of his depth. Not that we are talking about electorates any longer.

Voters are way, way down on the list of considerations in this new ball game. But perhaps you find yourself convinced, in the present economic circumstances, that there are no national crises any more, only global ones - and that the governing of all nations must now be subsumed under some overarching international framework of law and supervision, to be monitored and policed by suitably empowered agencies. Maybe you think that is an acceptable price to be paid for stability at home and security abroad. But consider this: what if the new dispensation, once installed, fails to produce that stability and security, or delivers it only to certain nations (not yours), or does so only by limiting freedoms that you consider precious? What recourse will you have then to remove it peaceably from power, as you do your national government?"

As the bishops have led, the Catholic laity have followed. The Knights of Columbus, a 1.7 million member Catholic fraternal organization, passed a resolution on August 6 at their 2009 general convention expressing "deep appreciation to the Holy Father for the timely publication of the encyclical Caritas in Veritate." Vatican apologist Robert Moynihan, founder and editor of Inside the Vatican magazine, a staunchly conservative publication, stood with the African bishops in their acceptance of Benedict's version of global governance, and dismissed critics as "doing the work of the devil."

On October 24, he said, "the Africans are supporting a more just 'world order,' something which the Pope also called for in his recent encyclical, not because they want a 'one world government' which might be a prelude to a type of 'anti-Christian' rule (the rule of anti- Christ), but precisely because there is already a 'world mis-government' which allows enormous injustices to be perpetrated with impunity. This leads to another thought: those who would encourage simple, good Catholics, and others, to fear that the Pope is calling for a dangerous, anti-Christian 'new world order' are being duped. The Pope knows that there already is a dangerous 'world government' (or 'mis-government') which is ... allowing the rape of Africa, and even encouraging it. So, those who are fanning the passions of the simple against any calls for a government which could restrain these excesses, are playing the devil's game. The type of 'world governance' the Pope was calling for is the same type these bishops are calling for: a reasonable government, with reasonable laws, able and willing to impede and prosecute these crimes against humanity. Until such a government is formed, to reign [sic] in the excesses already occurring, 'anti-Christian' forces will continue to have their day, and simple people will continue to suffer."

Such is the counterattack that Church apologists are likely to make against traditional Christians who reject Benedict's embrace of political globalism. Tony Blair, who converted to Catholicism in late 2007 after completing his ten-year term as Prime Minister of the UK, praised Caritas in Veritate in an August 27, 2009 speech to an annual assembly of members of Communion and Liberation, a Catholic "new ecclesial movement." Blair, like Benedict, believes that the Church should have a strong voice in politics and global governance. More than 10,000 members of the movement, which has a reputation for orthodoxy and loyalty to the Vatican, gave Blair two standing ovations. Blair (who has been a public supporter of "the right to choose") said, "The danger is clear: that pursuit of pleasure becomes an end in itself. It is here that Faith can step in, can show us a proper sense of duty to others, responsibility for the world around us, can lead us to, as the Holy Father calls it, "Caritas in Veritate."

Bankers have followed the lead of churchmen, and have praised Caritas in Veritate - while defending their own wealth and privilege. On October 21, 2009, Archbishop Vincent Nichols of Westminster organized a private seminar at which chairmen and CEOs from banks and other financial institutions met to study Caritas in Veritate. (The financiers in attendance included Schroders chief executive Michael Dobson, Schroders president George Mallinckcrodt, vice chairman of Goldman Sachs International Lord Brian Griffiths, Rothschild's director Anthony Salz, Barclays Bank chairman Marcus Agius and former Chief of the Defense Staff Field Marshal Lord Peter Inge.)

7

POPE FRANCIS - THE JESUIT CONDUIT

On February 11, 2013, Pope Benedict XVI announced his resignation. The news shocked the world as this was the first pope to step down in 600 years. That same day the BBC reported that lightning struck St. Peter's Basilica. Adding another dose of mysticism, 13 days later Cardinal Jorge Mario Bergoglio, S.J., Archbishop of Buenos Aires, Argentina is elected the new pope by the conclave of Cardinals on March 13, 2013. He takes the name Francis and becomes Pope Francis. In Biblical numerology 13 and 11 are negative numbers and are associated with the Devil and rebellion. In Revelation, it is the 13th chapter that introduces the final world empire and the Antichrist who heads it as the Beast. It also introduces the false prophet who performs miracles and supports the Beast.

It is in the 13th chapter we are given the numerical riddle identifying the Antichrist by the number of his name and his number is 666. The False Prophet breathes life into the image of the beast and causes all to worship it. This takes us to our next number. Pope Francis is now the 266 pope, which is one six shy of 666, and 66 represents Nebuchadnezzar's idolatrous golden image in the book of Daniel, which Babylonians were forced to worship. It was 6 cubits high and 6 cubits wide and foreshadows Revelation 13's idol. Incidentally, the practice of Satanism and the founding of the Church of Satan began in 1966.

In Satanism both 13 and 11 are numbers, which identify the devil. Numerology is an inherent part of

Satanism. The number 11 represents the sign of Aries, the 11th sign of the Zodiac and its symbol of the water bearer who is represented by Belial, a name of the Devil mentioned 16 times in the Old Testament and one time by Paul in his letter to the Corinthians. Men or women who committed the most evil, rebellious deeds were called children of, sons or daughters of Belial. Aries is also symbolized by the ram, which lines up with the two horned lamb of Revelation, which is a young ram. Jesus is depicted in the Bible as the lamb and the False Prophet as the young ram. The number 13 is long associated with the Devil and is used throughout Satanism. The Tarot death card is the 13th card.

The sudden change in papal leadership and the mystical details have many evangelicals wondering if Pope Francis is significant for Bible Prophecy, and if, in fact, he is the false prophet. Others reference the Prophecies of Popes, which states that there will be a last pope Peter the Roman, who will help usher in Armageddon. The Beast who rises from the sea has ten horns, which are ten kings. The little horn of Daniel is the Antichrist, and all 11 horns represent heads of countries and political leaders. The false prophet has two horns like a lamb. Like Jesus who is represented by a lamb, Revelation's lamb with horns signifies a religious leader but one that is in sheep's clothing. He appears to be a lamb but is not.

Horns in the Revelation and the book of Daniel symbolize leaders of countries. The pontiff fits the role of the false prophet because his first horn represents his leadership of the Catholic church. His second horn depicts the Pope as the Sovereign of Vatican City State. Vatican City was established as an independent state in 1929 by the Lateran Treaty. Vatican City is the world's smallest country and it functions like any other country even issuing its own coins. The Euro became the official currency of Vatican City in 2002. It is a microstate, which means it lies within a larger country within the European Union. The head of Vatican City is the pope. Thus the two horns can represent his being the head of the vast Catholic church and of his country, Vatican city. The two horns can also signify the false prophet's leadership of his church and his position with the Antichrist.

The false prophet's two horns in addition to the 11 horns of the 10 kings and little horn of the Antichrist give us a total of 13 horns that in total represents the beast, which again is a number of the devil. The Beast rises from the sea while the False Prophet is a beast who rises from the earth. Aleteia the Worldwide Catholic Network from Rome reported that Pope Francis is a pope "from the ends of the earth," coincidence?

Pope Francis is 76 years old, born on 17 December 1936 in Buenos Aries. His parents are Italian, and they migrated to Argentina in the 1920s. The pope speaks fluent Italian because of his Italian heritage. After obtaining a degree as a chemical technician, he chose the priesthood and entered the seminary of VillaDevoto. The Huffington Post reported that the pope proposed to his childhood sweetheart Amalia Damonte when he was 12. When she refused his proposal, he told her that if he didn't marry her, he was going to join the priesthood, and he did. On 11 March 1958, he moved to the novitiate of the Company of Jesus where he finished studies in the humanities in Chile. He went onto earn a degree in philosophy and from 1964 to 1966, he taught literature and psychology at two separate colleges. He then went on to study and earn a degree in theology in the St. Joseph major seminary of San Miguel. On 13 December 1969, he was ordained a priest. In looking over his career, we find that on the 13th day during the month, he is ordained a priest and elected pope.

Cardinal Jorge Mario chose the name Francis after Francis of Assisi who founded the Franciscan order and who devoted himself to a life of poverty while preaching repentance. Francis upon seeing a vision, became the first to receive the stigmata. He said that absolute personal and corporate poverty was the essential lifestyle for the members of his order. He believed that nature itself was the mirror of God. He called all creatures his "brothers" and "sisters," and even preached to the birds. He is often portrayed with a bird, in his hand. On November 29, 1979, Pope John Paul II declared St. Francis to be the Patron of Ecology. According to Fox News, the pope picked Francis because he was immediately inspired to take the name of St. Francis of Assisi because of his work for peace and the poor and was prompted by a cardinal friend upon his election not to forget the poor.

In addition to being the first Latin American pope and Francis in the pontificate, he is also the first Jesuit Pope. Jesuits are known for their free thinking and intellectual contributions. Since the inception of the order, Jesuits have been teachers. Today, there are Jesuit-run universities, colleges, high schools and middle or elementary schools in dozens of countries. Jesuits also serve on the faculties of both Catholic and secular schools as well. 28 Jesuit colleges and Universities exist in the US alone.

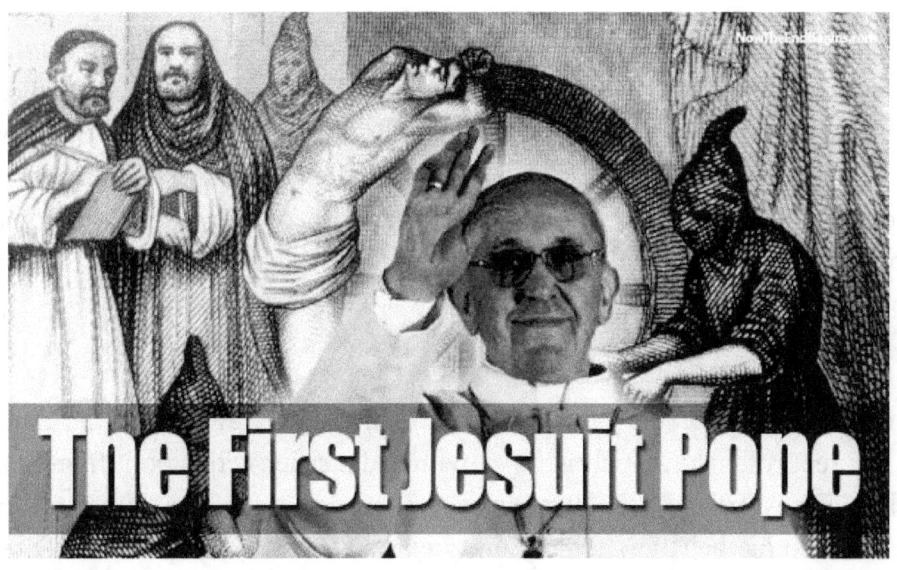

Jesuits are also known for their involvement in publications, and most Jesuit colleges and universities have their own presses, which produce a variety of books, book series, textbooks and academic publications. Their theological free thinking is academically oriented and prevalent at the university level. Jesuits in Latin America received a bad reputation among evangelicals In Latin America because of their development of liberation theology, a highly controversial movement condemned by Pope John

Paul II on several fundamental aspects. Liberation theology is essentially Christianized Marxism. The Peruvian Roman Catholic priest Gustavo Gutierrez first used the term in 1973. It proposed that the Gospels demanded that the church concentrate its efforts on liberating the world's people from poverty and oppression. They adopted Marxist ideas, supported revolutionary movements and criticized traditional church institutions. They espouse that Christians must work for social and economic justice for all people. Essentially liberation theology is a form of Christian communism and based on the view that the teachings of Jesus Christ compel Christians to support communism as the ideal governmental system. Christian communists believe that the Apostles practiced communism and that it was taught by Jesus who they hail as the first Marxist.

There are conflicting stories that when Pope Francis was Provincial Superior of the Jesuits in Argentina. he was accused of not having protected two priests who were kidnapped, which the Holy See denies. CNN reported that in 1976, during Argentina's dictatorship, the navy kidnapped priests Orlando Yorio and Francisco Jalics. It was suggested that he was partly responsible for the priests' prolonged detention, The human rights group Center for Legal and Social Studies in Argentina actually opposed Francis' selection as pope. CNN also reported that it was even alleged that Francis lied under oath during an investigation into the theft of babies from prisoners during the dictatorship. Francis testified that he never knew about the baby-stealing until after the dictatorship had fallen. An interviewed victim claims that Francis knew about it at the time. She said she had written to Francis about it. Upon his election there are already hints of a possible dark side to Pope Francis.

Pope Francis has gained notoriety for humility and shunning of the pomp and circumstance that go with being pope, such as his refusal to wear the red mozzetta, standing to receive the Cardinals versus sitting on the papal throne, and taking the minibus with the other Cardinals instead of the papal car. This may even more so be evidence of a maverick, which is not uncommon for a free-thinking intellect to act. If he begins to produce miracles, we might very well have on our hands the emergence of the false prophet, which only time will tell. The pope would need to be a maverick to team with the Antichrist, if the False Prophet is in fact this pope.

It is not geopolitically unforeseeable given the institutional political seat of the Antichrist, which is revealed later in this report for the Antichrist to sit with and partner with a pontiff and for them to form a special relationship. The Antichrist will introduce a strange god and names himself as one and the false prophet will advocate on his behalf. The possibility exists for an evil pope to condone the destruction and persecution of the church as he campaigns for the Antichrist.

The next question is how will this pope continue where other popes have left off in their influence in the European Union? This pope in that he is a Jesuit will most likely be more active than previous popes in relation to the politics of the Union. The Guardian named him the radical from Flores, who will reshape the Catholic Church. Domingo Bresci, a priest who studied with Bergoglio in the 50s and later worked with him in Flores and who is now an adviser in the government's religious affairs bureau and a prominent figure in the leftist Liberation Theology movement, said the new pope was not a person to take half measures. Bresci said the world should brace for a transformation of one of its oldest and most conservative religions. He added, .He is going to have an impact on the world; he'll change the power structure of the church and challenge the ostentatious pomp of the Vatican."

Bergoglio demands discipline. When he was made vicar general of Flores in 1992, he insisted that church authorities reveal the properties they owned. When he became archbishop, he reshuffled the clerics who opposed him. Those who know him said Pope Francis is likely to do the same in the Vatican by clearing out the dominant old guard of Cardinals. "Slowly and strategically, he will introduce changes as he becomes more powerful and others become weaker. Bresci, predicted the transformation to be the biggest in half a century or more. "He will be strict on finance. There will be zero tolerance of sexual abuse and homosexual liaisons by priests. This is his style. It comes from Flores."

The Commission of the Bishops' Conferences of the European Community (COMECE), made up of Bishops delegated by the 26 Catholic Bishops' Conferences of the European Union, which examines EU policy and legislation from a Catholic perspective and maintain a regular dialogue with EU institutions stated after the election of Pope Francis:

"At this critical time when there is deep confusion about Europe's future, it may be an opportune moment for the new pontiff to inject fresh enthusiasm into the search for a vision of Europe. This vision enshrines those Christian values, which so inspired the founding fathers of the European project.

The Apostolic Exhortation Ecclesia in Europa, which Pope Francis' predecessor John Paul II published ten years ago still has a powerful message for those working to shape the Europe of tomorrow. We feel sure that the Successor of Peter will recognize with pride what has been achieved together by the European nations and encourage Europe's political leaders - and incidentally all of us at COMECE - to continue, with solidarity and respect for subsidiarity, on the path towards unity in diversity for all within the European family"

Unity in diversity is the official motto of the EU and right out of the tenets of European federalism, which sprang from Catholic thought. It is the wine in the cup of the Whore spoken of in Revelation Chapter 17, which this report exposes in detail. If this pope is not the False Prophet, which time will reveal, we can at the least expect Pope Francis- this Jesuit pope- to embrace federalist ideology, and help lead the governments and peoples of the world to its final one-world destination and further have its influence on the evolving European Union

8

RETURN OF THE EMPIRE

The European Union's "Parliament" Building in Strasbourg has been deliberately designed to represent the Tower of Babel, as per the famous painting by Peter Brueghel, painted in 1563. The logic behind this symbolism is the European Union is seeking to "build the house of Europe" - a task yet to be completed. The building is complete and in use, but is designed to look unfinished, and even has ringed platforms around it to represent scaffolding. When asked by a secular journalist 'why the Tower of Babel?' an EU official replied, 'What they failed to complete 3000 years ago - we in Europe will finish now.'

FEDERALISM

At this time when the EU is at the crossroads of punching up to its weight, making its presidency more visible on the world stage and implementing the various details of the Lisbon Treaty, meant to transform the EU into a political power, the Spinelli Group of federalists recently formed with the intention of driving the EU forward politically. The cast of names comes as no surprise, that it is headed by Guy Verhofstadt who also heads the ALDE group of liberals in the EU parliament and who stated in his article, "The Financial Crisis Three Ways Out For Europe," that the start of the Great Recession in 2008 ended the US's lead role in a bipolar world and ushered in a multipolar world and age of empires for which the EU exists as one of its poles.

THE OVERLOOKED POWER GROUP

Bible Scholars agree that the final world power will rule globally. The Scripture states that the entire world worships the Beast and he institutes his Mark worldwide. End time watchers follow developments in globalization and the New World Order. Unfortunately, around this premise many conspiracy theories have arisen teaching that secret societies are planning for world dominion. The Masons, the Illuminati, the Trilateral Commission, the Catholic Church, the Jewish elite, the Bilderbergers are among the groups planning the takeover. Each theory claims to document their facts on insider's revelations and sound research.

While looking for the secret society, these end-time watchers have failed to discover a European think-tank whose members belong to a political ideological movement which do not operate in secret but out in the open and have influenced the European Union's evolution. Their teachings provide a blueprint for global rule. These individuals believe in European "federalism"-the ideological term for one-worldism. The movement began in the late 1930's in Britain, as a solution to the World War. In this proposed solution, the US federal government's model would govern on a worldwide scale. The "federalist papers," which drew their inspiration from English federal thought, inspired many writers and works on the topic from 1910 onward. The Round Table, a well-known political publication, advocated federalizing the British Empire.

In 1929, a New Europe Group proposed a European federation with a common currency, and foreign and defense policies. In 1939, the federalists published the Federalist Union Manifesto. They sought out activists by sending letters to those in the Who's Who interested in world affairs. Federalists believe that a nation's sovereignty is artificial, and that there can be no hope for international order while nations act independently. A writer stated that "unless we destroy the sovereign state, the sovereign state will destroy us," and they envision a world order which limits national sovereignty. They insist that federal union will take the globe's governments from the nation-state to the world-state, which would be an evolutionary advance. The ultimate aim of federalism is world government, for they view federalism as the antithesis of totalitarianism. Supporters of federalism proposed that "the long-term aim of Federal Union remains the establishment of a world federation." Their more immediate aim was "the promotion of a democratic federation of Europe as part of the post-war settlement."

During these early years, author and lecturer Lionel Robbins sketched the outline of a new world order. He suggested that Europe become a federation of states, consenting to limited sovereignty while pursuing a common trade policy. His proposals foreshadowed what the European Union later accomplished. The formation of the European Community occurred in line with federalist thinking. Although these policies duplicate what occurred in the historical account of the European Union's formation, the federalists did not initiate its creation. Jean Monnet is responsible for the EU's formation.

In 1944, the group established the European Union of Federalists (EUF). They associated themselves with the worldwide movement for world federal government. Today in Washington exists the headquarters of the World Federalist Association which in 2004 became the Democratic World Federalists. This group enlists the Hollywood crowd, and is a branch of the liberal left. They embrace Mother Earth rhetoric. Environmental issues, which leaders view as a global crisis, support their argument for international law.

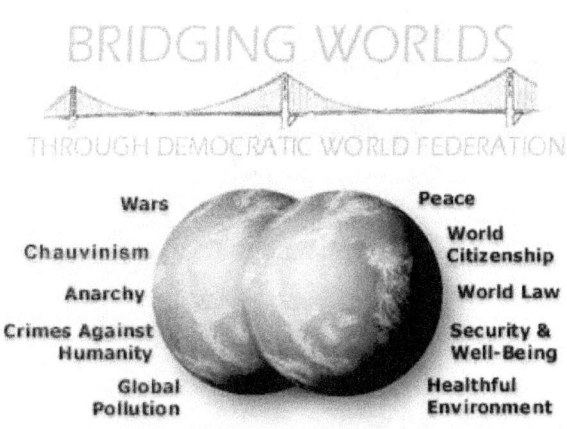

Federalist slogans include "Peace Through World Law," "One Planet-One People," and "One Earth Needs World Federation." World Federalists seek to strengthen the UN as a prospect for world government. They applaud the EU's endeavors. The European federalists lead the movement by enlisting political leaders and intelligentsia; in addition, they publish sophisticated journals propagating their ideology.

THE FEDERALIST MOVEMENT, JEAN MONNET AND THE EU'S FORMATION

When nuclear bombs fell on Hiroshima and Nagasaki in 1945, the urgency of the federalists' desire for action became more intense than ever. For many, this meant action on a world scale. Federalist groups now existed throughout the world. The Federal Trust for Education and Research formed in 1945 in London. The Trust's activity involved itself with the European Union, as a route to its wider agenda. Stalin ordered a total blockade of Berlin in 1948, impelling Europeans to unite. That summer, World Federalists held their second congress in Luxembourg. Emery Reves, one of the speakers, began to see European federation as a possible step toward world federation, in line with federalist policy. Federalists endorsed regional integration as "an approach to world federation." The long-term goal of "world government" seemed less immediate and practical than action on a smaller, more limited front, either in Europe or across the Atlantic.

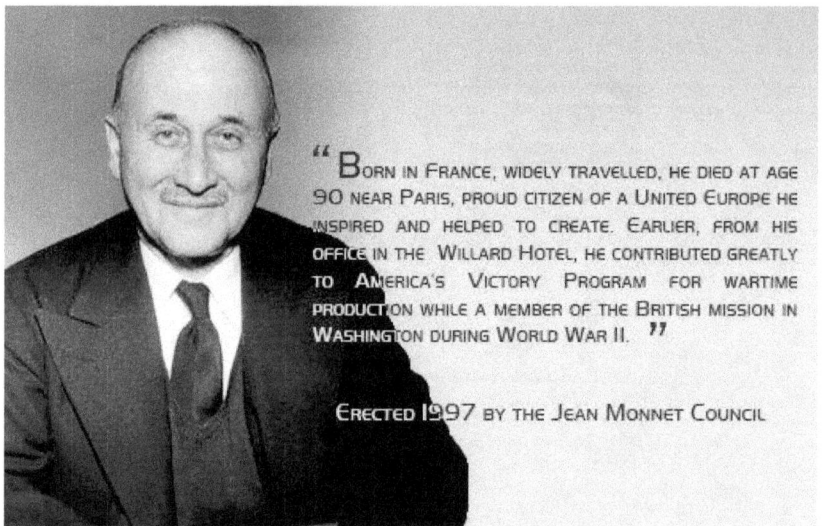

The federalists sought to improve and strengthen world institutions such as the United Nations, the International Monetary Fund, and the World Bank. These globalists ranked first in undertaking the work of turning the UN into an effective world authority. While these efforts failed, Jean Monnet reiterated their vision for the European Union. Federalists viewed the EU as an indirect route to achieve their end.

On April 18, 1951, European leaders signed the European Coal and Steel Treaty in Paris. The treaty's members included France, Germany, Italy, Belgium, Luxembourg, and the Netherlands. That same year, an editorial in Federal News declared: "Just as European Federalists have rightly said that it will be impossible to build a world federation without first federating Europe, it is now becoming clear that it may not be possible to federate Europe without doing so as part of a wider scheme of federation."

Federalists declared that Federal Union should not advocate the setting up of any specific federation, but should encourage the establishment of any federations and international organizations that would tend to lead to ultimate world federation.

Monnet, with the Benelux statesman Paul-Henri Spaak and Jean Beyen, worked on a plan for the reformation of Europe, which took clear form in 1955. The foreign ministers of the six member countries met in Messina, Sicily. They launched the process that ended with the establishment of the European Community and EURATOM (European Atomic Energy Community) on January 1, 1958. The six decided to create a specialized community based on the ECSC, (European Coal and Steel Community) for the peaceful development of nuclear energy. At the same time, they decided to remove trade barriers and create a common market in which goods, persons, and capital could move freely. On March 25, 1957, European leaders signed the EURATOM (European Atomic Agency) Treaty and the European Economic Community (EEC) or Common Market Treaty in Rome on Capitoline Hill. The EU's founders viewed economic union as the prerequisite for eventual political integration.

The EEC's institutional structure, laid out in the Treaty of Rome, was federalist in character. The resemblance was not coincidental; Altiero Spinelli, an Italian federalist, influenced de Gasperi in the writing of the treaty. He wrote Monnet's speech for his inaugural address as the first president of the EEC's High Authority. The widespread acceptance of federalist thinking in the six ECSC countries in the early 1950's ensured the approval of their logic by politicians and the public.

In 1957, with the signing of the Rome Treaties, the Trust's European activities expanded. Membership grew, and a wide range of expert speakers became available to the Trust including people from the EU Commission and the member countries. The subjects soon covered such specialized fields as agriculture, financial investment, transport, labor law, and tax. The Trust developed the reputation as a significant organization. One of the speakers, Fernard Braun, a young commission official, later became the Director-General in charge of the program to complete the international market by the end of 1992.

Europeans historically regard Jean Monnet as the father of Europe, the father of the common market. Born in 1888 to a family of wine growers, Jean Monnet long remained anonymous despite his accomplishments. He was neither a politician nor a technocrat. He had no particular expertise in any field, although some experts listed him as an economist.

In 1919, the Treaty of Versailles established the League of Nations. Monnet became the League's Deputy Secretary General. Europe experienced the devastation of two world wars and faced the dictatorships of Hitler and Mussolini Economic crisis and unemployment marked postwar Europe, while both the United States and the Soviet Union emerged in much stronger positions. Monnet believed that the countries of Europe should unite to bring freedom and prosperity to their continent. He argued that national sovereignty was outmoded if it prevented Europe from keeping pace with the times in the age of the superpowers.

During the Kennedy era, growth in the EU slackened due to de Gaulle's nationalism and anti-American sentiments. He called the US, "the unwanted federator of an integrated Europe." To refute this, Kennedy called for a joint interdependence. In 1963, Kennedy's speech in St. Paul's Church of Frankfurt expressed satisfaction with a United Europe. He stated:

"It would be a world power, capable of dealing with the US on equal footing in every domain."

After de Gaulle's departure, Jean Monnet's idea of building up the European Union as a partner of the United States gained popularity. European federalists began to consider how a federal Europe might help to build a wider union of democracies, as a step on the long road to world federation. David Barton, in an article in World Affairs, gave a more exact meaning to the term "Atlantic Community." Essentially, he saw it "as linking militarily, politically and economically large trading blocs or regional groupings." He believed these would serve as an example for other regions, and could finally lead to a world community.

Although the Federalist Trust focused on the EU, Jean Monnet, its true founder, did not follow a federalist blue-print. In 1976, the European Council made Jean Monnet an "Honorary Citizen of Europe." In March of 1979, Monnet died. As the European Document entitled "Jean Monnet, a Grand Design For Europe," states: His message has the force of all simple ideas. Instead of wasting time and energy in trying to apportion blame for a horrific war, the countries of Europe should combine to bring freedom and prosperity to their continent. The imperative of the age was to bring economies together, to merge interests, to make the means of production more efficient in a world dominated by competitiveness and progress. Monnet's message went to the root of national sovereignty which he argued was outmoded if it prevented Europe from keeping pace with the times in the age of superpowers.

FEDERALIST INFLUENCE IN THE EU'S EVOLUTION

By 1966, the Trust's focus shifted toward the Community's economic, institutional, and political development. Those attending its conferences began to include a wider range of policy-makers and Community watchers. By the late 1960s, the Trust studied ways to improve Community institutions and policy. Federalists began thinking in terms of a common set of foreign, security, defense, and monetary policies.

Many of the staff members of Federal Union regarded European federalism as the first step in establishing a new world system. Most of them later became prominent in their various occupations. Some became members of the EU Commission, some became editors for European affairs journals, and still others held other influential posts. Former French President Valery Giscard d'Estaing spoke at Federal Trust conferences before his presidency.

- In 1973, Britain, Denmark, and Ireland joined the Community, bringing the number of Member States to nine.

- On January 1, 1981, Greece became the community's tenth member.

- On January 1, 1986, Spain and Portugal became the Community's next two members, bringing the number of Member States to twelve.

EU countries in the early 1980s suffered high unemployment and low growth. Europe barely recovered from the 1982 recession, unlike the US this sparked renewed commitment.

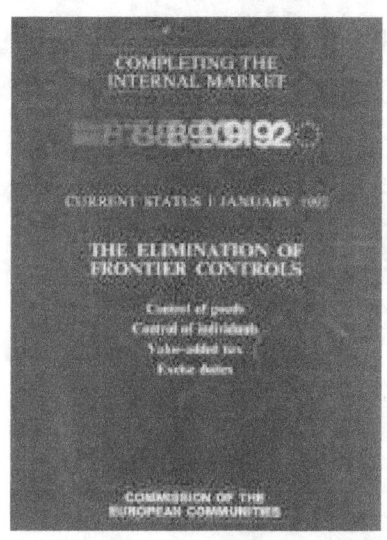

European leaders felt it imperative to reconstruct their economies, provide a large base for their companies to compete in the global marketplace. Two major decisions helped them to accomplish this go First, in June 1985, the Community published a white paper entitled "Completing the Internal Market." It contained 285 directives and spec regulations, and assigned each directive an expected date of adopt ranging from 1985 to 1991. The directives removed fiscal, technical, a physical barriers and harmonized product standards, diplomas, insurance and credit regulations, as well as differences in taxation from country to country throughout the Community.

The second major decision, the European Single Act, came into force on January 1, 1987. Under the Act, a yes vote by the Council of Ministers only called for a weighted majority, except in cases involving health and environmental issues. In the past, all decisions made by the Council required voting by unanimous decision. This method slowed the EU's growth. The EU could now move forward.

In 1987, the Trust examined the idea of a European Security Community. The group's report proposed that the Union pool their defense forces. The European Union would become the partner of the United States as the European pillar of the Atlantic Alliance. It would seek a common security relationship with the Soviet Union while reforming the United Nations into a more effective peacekeeper. The report views the Union as a kind of world community made up of regional communities, as a stage in the progression toward the more distant prospect of a world government. The Trust produced a set of proposals on how the Community might develop into a Union with federal institutions. They suggested instituting a European federal bank to underpin economic and monetary union. The Trust also proposed a common security and foreign policy. The Union adopted all of these proposals, and they are now Union policy. The European Central Bank under the Lisbon Treaty became an official EU institution.

- In 1995, Austria, Sweden and Finland became members of the Union bringing the number of
- Member States to 15.
- In 2004, 10 new countries, the Czech Republic, Estonia, Hungary, Latvia, Lithuania, Poland, Slovakia, and Slovenia, plus the Mediterranean islands of Malta and Cyprus joined the Union.
- In 2007, Romania and Bulgaria followed bringing the number of EU Member States to 27.

Federalists believe that sovereign nations are no longer able to solve the world's problems. They regard national sovereignty as a traditional governmental precept of the past. Former NATO General Secretary Manfred Worner stated: "If Europe is to measure up to its new responsibilities-and it has no choice-it must-then it will have to pull itself together rapidly and free itself of outmoded notions of sovereignty." The Belmont European Policy Centre in Brussels, a European think-tank made this statement: "On May 1950, the Schuman Declaration proclaimed that the so-called sovereign nation state no longer constituted a satisfactory model for organizing relations between European states. Only through pooling specific elements of sovereignty could they prevent further catastrophes and regain their ability positively to influence their nations' destinies."

Franz Anderiessen, former Vice President of the EU Commission, declared: "Europe, and the world at large have suffered immeasurably, not least in this enlightened century, from exaggerated ideas of the role of the sovereign states." The European Commission in part funds the New Federalist, the newsletter of the Young European Federalists. An eminent member of the World Federalists in the United States commented in an essay, which appeared in the newsletter: "The current nation-state system is impractical and, in many ways, a global anarchy...Presently, blind, idolatrous nationalism is the primary force in opposition to world federation. Children at a young age must be taught the importance of loyalty to one's family, community and homeland… loyalty to one's planet must also be emphasized. Is there a better way than war and economic coercion to solve the world conflict? Yes, a better alternative is through system of equitable and enforceable world law"

Federalists aim for a new world based on the rule of international law, thus achieving Pax Universalis. To the federalist, one's loyalty belongs to planet Earth. Urgency accompanies their cause, with the slogan "mankind must unite or perish." Some members believe federalism is a force that will be unleashed throughout the whole world. They view global unity as the utopian solution to end all wars. Federalists believe that with the collapse of communism, their goal for world government has become a concrete and political aim. In this age when threats can be global in nature, nations will find no other alternative but to align with one another. Federalism's precepts have humanistic aims. The New Federalist summed up the ideology for international law in stating that:

"Federalism overcomes the cause of war: the division of the world into sovereign states with the world federation, that final stronghold of violence between men, war, will be eliminated: international anarchy will be replaced by the rule of law between states. The world federation will, as Kant taught us, open up a world in which man can consider other men as ends in themselves and in which he can fully and autonomously develop all the capacities that are within him. The world federation will open the history of the human race" We know from Scripture that the world federation will not open the history of the human race but rather end it. The Antichrist will use this ideology to gain dictatorial control over the world.

THE GLOBAL AGENDA

A center of power must emerge with the capability of supporting the plan for a world democratic order. The European Union could be such a power....It is reasonable to believe that Europe will hold sufficient power to relieve the United States of some of their overwhelming world responsibilities, and thus have the authority to persuade them to support the democratic reform of the United Nations.

GLOBALIZATION

Along with the one-world government movement, social, economic, and political trends are bringing about the unification of the globe. Even religion follows the global path through organizations such as the World-Wide Council of Churches.

With today's technology, no one nation remains isolated. Television satellites, fax machines, and data banks bring many countries together in the transference of information. Technology has made the world a smaller, more unified place. While Globalization is a process, technological developments act as the catalyst that speeds it along. Payment systems of major countries closely interlink. Banks around the globe communicate electronically. The Economist stated: "Today's economies are interdependent and interconnected. Flows of trade and capital tie countries more closely together than at any time since the 19th century. A recession in one country slows growth elsewhere. One government's budget deficit draws resources not just from domestic savings but from a global pool of capital that all have to share."

In addition to economic and financial interdependence, the world is breaking up into regional groupings of nations that act as trade blocs. As twenty to thirty nations form one of these blocs, they become a section of the globe. As the world coalesces into sections, unification becomes a simpler process. Five or six parts of a pie join easily, compared to over 160 pieces of a puzzle. The Great Recession showed the impact of globalization the day the American financial markets plummeted. The European markets followed and caused a ripple effect hitting every major market around the globe. Within days major financial papers reported that the world economy had literally come to a stop.

National problems that have a worldwide impact such as the Great Recession, nuclear arms buildup, the environment, and drugs, have prompted nations to intensify their efforts to work together in their common causes. Banks even unite internationally to fight computer crime and money laundering.

The Earth Summit of 1992 brought together nations from around the globe to coordinate global environmental policy. This Summit involved nearly four times as many countries as founded the United Nations. Maurice Strong, the Secretary General for the United Nations Conference on Environment and Development, felt that environmental problems such as global warming, the ozone hole, acid rain, soil degradation, and deforestation jeopardized all nations, and because of this he stated that "the world has now moved beyond economic interdependence to ecological interdependence-and even beyond that to an intermeshing of the two. The world's economic and earth's ecology are now interlocked-'unto death do them part,' to quote one of Canada's industrial leaders. This is the new reality of the century, with profound implications for the shape of our institutions of governance, national and international."

WORLD INSTITUTIONS

During World War II, world leaders recognized the need for international economic institutions. In 1944, political leaders established the International Monetary Fund and the World Bank. The General Agreement of Tariffs and Trade (GATT) followed in 1948, along with a new wave of regional organizations. It instituted a code of rules by which countries could trade, as well as a forum for resolving disputes among trading partners. It aimed to liberalize world trade through the reduction of trade barriers, for free trade ensures peace among nations. Nations coordinate their trade policies through the GATT. The European Union advocated an international currency to replace the dollar and the yen, and a new international monetary system to underpin the GATT trade system. The Union stated that the GATT's ultimate objective is "a single world market." The European Union proposed the idea of a one-world monetary system in 1986, as an amendment to the GATT.

At the conclusion of the Uruguay Round in April 1994, over 120 countries signed an agreement in Marrakesh, Morocco, that created the World Trade Organization (WTO). The successor to the GATT, it acts as the United Nations of world trade, and continues to liberalize the global market. It began operation in January of 1995. The UN, founded with 51 Member States, now includes 192. The UN's peacekeeping role has broadened considerably in recent years. Since the end of the Cold War, the UN has involved itself in the settling of conflicts across the globe. Commenting on this development, The Economist stated: "For the first time the nations of the world, rich and poor, are beginning to cooperate for agreed ends on a scale that hitherto only idealists have even dreamed about."

Federalists aim to transform the United Nations into a democratic world federation. In 1991, a year before the Earth Summit, thirty-six respected world leaders put forth a document calling for a World Summit on Global Governance. The Stockholm Initiative aims to strengthen the UN so that it can better handle the global challenges of the future. It seeks to adopt a new approach to maintaining and developing international law. The proposed Commission on Global Governance seeks to strengthen the UN or form a new institution for the same purpose. Former European Commission President Jacques Delors suggested that the UN develop a "Council for Economic Security" to rewrite the rules for the global village. Delors saw it as unacceptable that single nations attempt to solve problems that have a worldwide scope.

The idea of having international rules echoes in many foreign affairs journals. Dennis Healy, Britain's former Defense Minister and Chancellor of the Exchequer, stated: "If we are talking about a new world order, I can only see a role for the UN. We can no longer tackle the great problems like environmental pollution, migration and global arms control, on a regional basis. International rules are required, especially when we remember that the population of the world is doubling every 50 years."

The International Monetary Fund (IMF), founded at the Bretton Woods Conference in 1944, secures global monetary joint action. It enlists 184 member nations. The Conference on Security and Cooperation, created in 1975, enlists 56 nations. Established as a regional organization of the UN Charter, it deals with security, human rights, and trade. Its job includes giving early warning of potential conflicts, improving crisis management, and developing military confidence-building mechanisms. Besides the CSCE, other regional organizations have sprung up since World War II.

End time watchers often look at the UN and various world institutions as the possible launching pad for the Antichrist. These institutions have no governmental powers. No single world institution has the power or capacity to govern the world. When one notes how the EU utilizes these institutions, and its future plans for them, one sees Scripture unfold before their very eyes.

The EU bases its policy and laws on those of global institutions. For areas of policy not covered by any of these organizations, the EU establishes its own regional ones. The Council of Europe deals with human rights, health, migration, law, culture, and the environment. All of these organizations use abbreviated letters or acronyms which are synonymous with the EU. Political leaders are negotiating and signing so many of these treaties that it would require an entire book to list and explain them all. These treaties form a web over the entire globe. With each new treaty, one more additional strand links nation to nation. Technological advances and infrastructures act as the bonding material holding them all together.

THE CORNERSTONE FOR UNITING THE WORLD

Within the EU, federalists hold key positions, and impact upon the EU's future direction and policies toward global governance. EU bureaucrats have adopted a federalist blueprint. With EU laws based on those of world institutions, once the EU becomes the world's leading power, it will lead other nations into global governance. In its mega superpower status, its policies will take precedence on the world stage. Lucio Levi, the editor of The Federalist Debate, published in Torino, Italy, stated in the July 2001 issue:

"A center of power must emerge with the capability of supporting the plan for a world democratic order. The European Union could be such a power....It is reasonable to believe that Europe will hold sufficient power to relieve the United States of some of their overwhelming world responsibilities, and thus have the authority to persuade them to support the democratic reform of the United Nations."

Federalists have already mapped out the route the EU will take to achieve world government. A powerful EU will have the greatest voice in world organizations. Most nations will hand over their sovereignty to these institutions. When the EU has sufficient power, it will write the rules for the world.

Italy has proposed that in the future the European Union might seek a single permanent seat at the UN Security Council. Germany's defense minister also supports the EU's having a single seat on the UN Security Council. These proposals are the first stage of what has yet to occur. The 1999 issue of The Federalist published in Pavia, Italy, states: *"It is as indicated, a question of predicting what type of world equilibrium the birth of the European federation will help to create, and what new forces it will help to unleash. We are all federalists because of our conviction that the founding of a European federation will be an important step forwards on the road towards the creation of a world federation, that it will allow the establishment of more stable, peaceful and open relations between peoples, that it will give the United Nations a more solid basis for action, that it will, through the example which its own birth will set the world, favor the development of new trends toward regional unification and give considerable impulse to the diffusion of the culture of the unity of mankind. And it will do this by mere virtue of its mere existence, and regardless of its governments' inclinations over foreign policy."*

Federalist thought provides the ideological backbone for the European Union. These ideals based on both religious and humanistic thinking and the teachings in the cup of the Whore provide the Antichrist with a perfect platform for world rule.

9

BUILDING AN EMPIRE

When Belgian Minister Louis Michel addressed the Belgian Foreign Affairs Committee, on November 12, 2002, he explained that the EU intended to incorporate the whole of North Africa and the Middle East, but also Russia. In other words, the entire northern half of Asia as far as Vladivostok, is to be incorporated into the EU. On October

13th 2008, the EU granted Morocco an "advanced association status." It is the first special association status granted by the EU to a third country and it is meant to be a step towards fully integrating Morocco in the EU. From October 13th 2008, the Moroccan minister of Foreign Affairs would be allowed to participate in the EU Foreign Affairs Council of Ministers and in other EU institutions such as Europol, the European Police Office, and Eurojust, the EU body dealing with judicial cooperation. Israel is said to be the next candidate to obtain a "special association status" with the EU.

THE TOWER OF EUROPE

A single world system is not new to man. Genesis records the historical account of the Tower of Babel. Mankind in ancient times united their efforts to build a tower to reach into the heavens. God declared that "now nothing that they propose to do will be withheld from them," and confounded their language. Give man too much power, and he becomes dangerous. A unified world with a single world government will be a modern-day Tower of Babel.

It is paradoxical that as the world grows more populated, it becomes more of a single unit. To date, we see the skeletal form of a one-world system, and can speculate on its continuing evolution. The world is breaking up into regional economic groupings. Pat Buchanan commented that "in the New World Order, rules are set by west and east globalists." These policy makers think in terms of international law as evidenced by the European Union federalists. World institutions will gain more power, and govern in their respective areas with the Antichrist as head of the European Union leading the world into oneness.

A one-world government will become man's final attempt at creating a utopian society that excludes God and deifies man. The one individual who will advocate and pursue this ideology will be man's greatest enemy. The world federation will not "open the history of the human race," but rather end it. The process of globalization is occurring through the natural order of events. At present, the world is fragmented. The European Union will act as the cornerstone for uniting the world, in the same way Jesus is the "chief cornerstone" of the church. None of this is coincidental; we know that the Antichrist's empire here on earth mimics the Kingdom of God.

Former Harvard Professor Samuel Huntington speculated in the 1990's that "the EC if it were to become politically cohesive would have the population, resources, economic wealth, technology and actual potential military strength to be the preeminent power of the 21st century." Cornelius van der Klugt, while he chaired Philips, affirmed: "If we organize ourselves, Europe will grow faster than the US and Japan combined." The EU is in the process of building its empire. According to Scripture, the EU will become the most powerful empire the world has ever known. EU bureaucrats purpose to transform the EU into a political world power. Former French President Francois Mitterrand stated: "From now until the turn of the millennium, we have ten years to win the race for Europeans. No institution should escape this critical examination, not the European Community, NATO, the Council of Europe or the CSCE. All should play their part." Former German Chancellor Helmut Kohl declared: "I am convinced this is going to be the decade of the Europeans."

One motive for European unity is to reclaim the limelight that virtually all of its member countries enjoyed during earlier periods of history. At the start of the Cold War, the US and Soviet Union became the leading world powers. Europe suffered the greatest share of the war's destruction. America aided in the rebuilding of Europe and provided for its defense through the North Atlantic Treaty Organization.

Although Europe and America stood alongside each other as strong allies, Europeans harbored ill feelings concerning certain American policies. Some Europeans desired a significant place on the world stage.

At the end of World War II, the European dream was reborn, and during the Cold War it crept along. Charles de Gaulle stated in his Memoirs that "Europe by confederation of its nations, can and must be for the well-being of its people, become the greatest political, economic and military and cultural power that ever existed." From the mid- to late 1980s, a spark rekindled, and the fall of the Berlin Wall added fuel to the fire. The end of the Cold War and the beginning of the New World Order marked a new era for Europe.

THE FIRST STEP TO POLITICAL UNION

The completion of the 1992 Common Market acted as the first step toward political union. The EU aimed to become an economic power on equal footing with the US and Japan. This proclamation underscores their ambition for attaining superpower status, as many of the member nations had in their history. With the completion of the 1992 program, an economically united Europe became the world's largest market and largest trader. Edward Heath, former British Prime Minister and an ardent federalist, affirmed: "All history tells us that economic reform is followed by political reform and that political power follows economic power." The Soviet Union and the United States demonstrated this. It will be the same with the European Community."

"We need a political union first and foremost. That means we must, step by step, cede responsibilites to Europe."
ANGELA MERKEL
GERMAN CHANCELLOR

Many individuals view the EU as a solely economic venture among European nations. Skeptics doubted that the EU would ever work together on an economic scale, let alone a political one. Peter Linton, a Brussels-based American consultant, warned that: "You [had] better be ready for the integration process that is moving ahead faster and farther than anyone has realized." He added that many Americans have yet to grasp the political significance of the process, and to take it very seriously. As evidence of the magnitude of the EU's potential for superpower status, Lester C. Thurow, MIT's best known economist, declared: "In the past half century, the world played by rules written mostly by Americans; in the next half century, the world will play by rules written mostly by Europeans."

While natural disasters are occurring with greater frequency, events on the international scene have experienced more dramatic changes in a shorter span of time than at any previous time in history. As a result, some experts now say that "a year is a long time in history." In three years' time, the Berlin Wall and the Soviet Empire collapsed, and Germany reunited, marking the end of Communism and the Cold War, and the beginning of the New World Order. For the first time, an international coalition fought a war in the Middle East. The Israeli-Arab Peace Conference began. Islamic Fundamentalism, resurgent nationalism, and many internal conflicts around the globe emerged. During this time, the European Union signed its treaty on political union.

With the rapid changes sweeping Europe, the Union decided it was time to "renew their vows, the marriage contract of the twelve." The EU's response to these changes was to accelerate integration within the EU itself. The revolutions in Eastern Europe turned 1992 from a time of economic reform into the beginning of a political transformation. The European Union would remain the stable, solid core around which Europe would rebuild itself. During an EU summit meeting in 1989, EU leaders declared that "at this time of profound and rapid change, the Community is and must remain a point of reference and influence. It remains the cornerstone of a new European Architecture."

In 1990, former European Commission President Jacques Delors told the European Parliament that the Community would move fast toward full political union, a full-fledged EU foreign policy, and deep institutional reform. He felt that events in the East and the danger of resurgent nationalism underscored the need for closer EU political integration. Delors believed that these events made it "impossible.to separate the Community's economic role from its political one."

Those in the Union feel that the EU is "now perceived as a major power and is expected to be a big-league player." During Jacques Delors, EU Commission presidency, he took advantage of every opportunity to strive for the unification of Europe. Concerning the Gulf Crisis, he commented, "It is a unique change for this Community to make the new qualitative leap which will make (it) the cornerstone of the greater Europe of tomorrow and.an actor of stature equal to its responsibilities on the world stage."

It seemed that whatever the event, European Union leaders called for the EU to take a greater political role in the world. These proclamations underscored their ambitions and role within the Union to help it evolve into a leading superpower. This was after all their intentions from early on in the Union's formation.

A SINGLE EUROPEAN CURRENCY

To be a truly single market with political clout in the world, Europe needed a single currency. The single most political act that the EU embarked on in addition to forming the Common Market was the decision to have its own currency. Political ambitions prompted the adoption of a single currency. Unionists viewed monetary union as the catalyst that would transform Europe's economic union into its political union.

Valery Giscard d'Estaing, former president of France and founder of the annual G7 summits, stated in an interview that the creation of the single currency would "be seen by people as a major political advance." He believed that monetary union would "induce a move toward a more organized political Europe." Former German Chancellor Helmut Kohl asserted that the accords signed in Rome would ultimately lead the continent to political union. He went on to state:

"One thing is certain, when this Europe ... has a common currency from Copenhagen to Madrid and from The Hague to Rome, when more than 350 million people live in a common space without border controls, then no bureaucrat in Europe is going to be able to stop the process of political unification."

Former French President Francois Mitterrand declared: "With a single currency (and other factors), Europe will have the means to affirm itself as the world's main power...It is not that we have ambitions to dominate, but together, we are already nearly the main commercial power in the world...together, on all markets in the world we will be at least as strong as the United States or Japan."

In 1979, the European Monetary System began to function. The EMS kept EEC currencies within a fixed exchange rate structure. At the same time, the twelve member nations strengthened and coordinated their economic and monetary policies. European leaders decided in 1989 that all currencies will join the exchange rate mechanism (ERM) of the European Monetary System (EMS) on July 1, 1990.

The EU bears striking similarities to the Old Roman Empire and added one more by having their own currency. The Economist even noted: "So Europe's future lies with monetary union? Perhaps, but this also a step back to the past. The Roman Empire remember had a single currency."

In 1987, the Belgians minted the first silver coins, aimed at the collectors' market only. Imprinted on the coins were twelve stars, symbolizing the nations of the European Union, and the bust of Emperor Charles V. He was born in the Belgian town of Ghent, and was crowned head of the Holy Roman

Empire in 1519. Europeans chose Charles V for the first ever European Currency Unit (ECU) because of the striking geographical similarity between the Common Market and the Holy Roman Empire.

Former Commission President Jacques Santer made monetary union a priority while he was president-elect in 1994. Despite the skeptics' negative views, Santer showed no signs of wavering. He firmly stated: "EMU is coming as decided and planned…. euro would be a strong currency. European countries can only be sure of making themselves heard on world monetary affairs if they have a single currency as powerful as the dollar and the yen."

Santer believed that the "euro will be a counterweight to the US dollar in the international financial system." Santer was convinced that the euro will give the Union political status; he stated that "in the years ahead it will be interesting to see how the euro will reinforce the European Union externally."

THE EUROPEAN CENTRAL BANK AND THE LAUNCH OF THE EURO

EU leaders determined that the launch of the euro would occur in three stages. The first stage occurred in 1990 when currencies joined the exchange rate mechanism (ERM) of the European Monetary System (EMS) in, 1990. The second stage two called for the creation of the European Central Bank. Based on the German Bundesbank, it is now one of the most important central banks and is responsible for monetary policy covering the 16 Member States of the Eurozone. The EU established it in 1998.

On January 1, 1999, the euro became legal tender. On July 1, 2002, national currencies ceased to be legal tender. Euro bills and coins became the traded currency. Andrew Crockett, while he was general manager of the Bank for International Settlements (BIS) in Basel, stated: "Monetary union in Europe holds the promise of profound change in international finance. The economies sharing the euro could face the world as the largest single currency area and the largest trading bloc."

Fred Bergsten, a leading US international economist who heads the Washington-based Institute for International Economics, believes that the "single currency in monetary union will become a fully equal partner of the United States in all economic terms." US finance officials are beginning to worry about how the single currency will affect the dollar's role as the world's dominant currency. Bergsten predicted that because the euro belongs to the world's second largest economy, "it will thus immediately become the world's second key currency."

In 2002 China's finance minister Xiang Huaicheng, commented that his government should consider buying more euros as soon as possible, so as to not be overly reliant on the US dollar in its foreign exchange reserves. China considers the euro important, and believes that it will someday be on equal footing with the US dollar. Xiang Huaicheng stated that "it is inevitable that the euro will become some countries' reserve currency." The euro has already become a key currency for trade. The euro will increase the Union's clout in world markets. The euro will develop into a global reserve currency, and will alter the power relationship between the US and Europe on monetary and fiscal issues. It will challenge the dollar's role as the world's key currency eventually overtaking it.

THE TREATY ON POLITICAL UNION

In April 1990, France and Germany launched the idea of a new Treaty on Political Union that would include foreign policy. That month, after a one-day summit meeting in Dublin, "The Community firmly, decisively, and categorically committed itself to political union," stated Charles Haughey, the Irish Prime Minister at the time. On December 15, 1990, the Council of Ministers met in Rome at an Intergovernmental Conference on Political Union (IGC). One year later in December 1991, at Maastricht, the Netherlands, the conference convened.

Maastricht's most solid achievement was the firm commitment to establish economic and monetary union (EMU) involving a single currency governed by a European Central Bank by 1999, which it accomplished. Along with monetary union, the treaty established the beginnings of a common defense component which would evolve with later treaties. Article J.4 of the Treaty on European Union added: "The common foreign and security of the Union, including the eventual framing of a common defense policy, which might in time lead to a common defense."

It paved the way to the creation of a distinct political identity. The Maastricht agreement marked the first step in adding a political dimension to the EU, and transforming it from an economic venture into a political reality. An objective of the Maastricht Treaty was for the EU to "assert its identity on the international scene. through the implementation of a common foreign and security policy." The Maastricht Treaty, a 189-page document, allowed the EU to forge common foreign and defense policies for the first time. Former French President Mitterrand affirmed: "For the first time in their history, the Union will act together in foreign policy."

Prior to Maastricht, the EU acted in the area of foreign policy through European Political Cooperation (EPC). This was the EU's process of consultation and common action among its members in the field of foreign policy. An EPC meeting brought together the Member States' highest officials, their foreign ministers, and the EU Commission. The confidential telex system (coreu) linked the twelve foreign ministries of the Member States, the EPC secretariat, and the Commission. It provided rapid and secure communications, and reduced the need for holding special ministerial meetings. Through its single, coherent approach, EPC aimed to maximize its influence in international affairs. Maastricht turned EPC into something more than a consultation club; it laid the foundation for a real government. The 1992 Maastricht Treaty changed the name of the European Communities to the European Union and gave the EU the formal title of "Union."

The Economist, commenting on the treaty, stated: "Believers in a federal Europe insist that the treaty lays down the main elements, if only in embryo, of a future European government, a single currency, common foreign and defense policy, a common citizenship and a parliament with teeth. It is just a matter of waiting they believe, for history to take its course."

Alan Sked, who chaired the Anti-Federalist League, made similar observations and brought out additional points. He stated in The European, a European newspaper that existed during the 1990s and provided excellent coverage of the evolving European Union, that after Maastricht:

The Commission is preparing to become the government of Europe, with Jacques Delors or his successor as executive president. He himself proposed such a scheme to the European Parliament in January 1990, and on June 4, 1992 the former Italian Foreign Minister, Emilio Columbo, introduced an outline Constitution for the European Union, drawn up by four professors. Chapter 4 of this simply stated: The Commission is the government of the Union....The Community is almost a state already. It has its own flag, its own anthem, its own driving license, its own diplomatic service, its own parliament, and its own supreme court. Maastricht will give it its own bank, currency, police force, data bases and army. A Committee of the Regions will be set up to help suppress nation states. All of Europe's leaders know exactly what is being planned: the creation of a centralized superstate. The EU leaders agreed to meet again in 1996, to work out a second treaty on political union. They hoped that the next treaty would complete the process that Maastricht started.

THE AMSTERDAM TREATY: In the summer of 1996, EU leaders met and concluded the intergovernmental conference that led to the signing of the Amsterdam Treaty. The treaty did not accomplish what many had hoped. US leaders could not agree on the issues that needed reorganization. This treaty was supposed to make many internal changes so that the Union could enlarge to include new members. The treaty created a representative to speak for the Union on foreign policy issues; the High Representative for Common Foreign and Security Policy which acted as a junior foreign minister. The Treaty of Amsterdam, signed on October 2, 1997, entered into force on May 1, 1999. It amended and renumbered the EU and EC Treaties, and EU leaders looked forward to meeting again immediately after the turn of the millennium. The Amsterdam Treaty strengthened Union's powers in foreign policy and judicial cooperation.

THE NICE TREATY: EU leaders met and negotiated the Treaty of Nice and signed it on February 26, 2001, as an amendment to the existing treaties. The Nice Treaty overhauled the institutions of the European Union in preparation for a union of twenty-seven Member States rather than fifteen.

This treaty also provided the EU with a military structure and staff. Most of the changes agreed upon at Nice concerned power sharing within the European institutions as the Union expands. The treaty, capped the number of seats in the European Parliament and the size of the commission, two of the European Union's leading institutions. The next chapter discusses them in further detail. The Treaty of Nice prepared for enlargement and added more competencies for the EU including employment policy and a common foreign and security policy to cement the Union's political union.

THE LAEKEN DECLARATION: On December 14 and 15, 2001, the European Council met in Laeken with the purpose of providing impetus to increase the momentum of integration. They adopted a declaration of their intention to achieve a simpler union, and one that would have more presence in the world. They initiated a convention run by Federalists V. Giscard d'Estaing, G. Amato, and Jean-Luc Dehaene to write the Constitution of the Union-which, unlike the US Constitution, would become the final treaty, encompassing all of the previous treaties. By October of 2002, the convention presented a draft treaty for the Union. Laeken addressed the transition to euro coins, enlargement, internal market issues, the September 11 attacks, and the Union's policies on combating terrorism, including their actions in Afghanistan and a declaration of their position in the Middle East. The Laeken Declaration asked: "What is Europe's role in this changed world? Does Europe not, now that it is finally unified, have a leading role to play in the new world order, that of a power able both to play a stabilizing role worldwide and to point the way ahead for many countries and peoples?" Laeken also issued its "Declaration on the Operational Capability of the Common European and Security and Defense Policy," and provided teeth to the military structure organized at Nice.

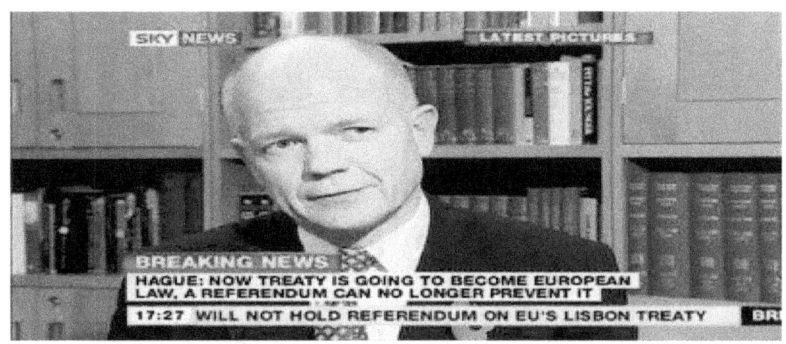

Former British Prime Minister Margaret Thatcher referred to the decisions made at Nice and Laeken as "one of the most ambitious political projects of our times." It should be noted that this "ambitious political project" began at the moment of the EU"s inception, for the primary aim of EU leaders has always been a political one, and those who viewed the EU as nothing more than an economic bloc are uninformed.

THE LISBON TREATY: In 2003, the EU drafted its Constitution and in 2004-2005, the EU Council approved the European Constitution (Treaty) and the Member States voted on it and rejected it. The European Council met in Lisbon for a new EU reform treaty (instead of a European constitution.) In 2007, EU leaders signed the Lisbon Treaty, which entered into force on December 1, 2009. The European Constitution merged into the Lisbon Treaty. The Lisbon Treaty amended previous EU treaties and is more modest than the previous constitutional project. The Charter of Fundamental Rights, which covers freedom and speech and religion, will legally bind 25 of the 27 EU Members. Britain and Poland obtained an opt-out.

Lisbon made changes to the EU institutions. The European Central Bank gained official status of being an EU institution along with the Council of Europe and the euro became the official currency of the Union. The Lisbon Treaty also renamed leading institutions. The High Representative for Common Foreign and Security Policy created by the Amsterdam Treaty was promoted to Vice President and

Foreign Minister of the Union along with other changes to help the 27 member union run smoothly, efficiently and to move it forward politically.

THE EUROPEAN ARMY

In order for the EU to become the powerful world empire outlined in the Scriptures, it must have a militia. The Antichrist's army conquers and treads down parts of the world. It lays siege to Israel, and assists in killing all who do not pay homage to the Antichrist.

Since 1946, several European nations have attempted to create military alliances. In 1948, the Brussels Treaty Organization (BTO) formed, but was absorbed by NATO in late 1950. In 1952, the newly established European Defense Community (EDC) attempted too much too soon, and it collapsed. In 1948, European leaders signed the Brussels Treaty-a modification of the EDC. It resulted in the Western European Union, which came into being in Paris on October 23, 1954, and ratified by all members in London on May 6, 1955. Its members included Britain and the six members of the EU. The WEU underwent significant changes.

In 1984 the European defense and foreign affairs ministers agreed to "reactivate" the WEU and harmonize the members' views on key issues. In 1987, the WEU Council adopted a "Platform on European Security Issues" and declared its intention to develop a "more cohesive European defense identity." During the 1987 oil shipping crisis in the Gulf, the WEU dispatched military forces-a sign that its vision of a cohesive identity had, in fact, become reality, due to the speed of world events, the WEU gained renewed interest. The end of the Cold War caused German unification, the end of the Warsaw pact, and uncertainty regarding NATO's role.

Prompted by the crisis in the Gulf and by German unification, which meant a larger, more powerful Germany and an uncertain NATO, the EU members decided that their union should include defense. Other potential threats include international terrorism, political instability in North Africa, and threats from the USSR, China, and the Middle East. Some suggested that the WEU merge with the EU.

At the time, Luxembourg's Foreign Minister Jacques Poos argued that the Gulf Crisis illustrated the urgent necessity of establishing a common European foreign and security policy. A spokesman for former French president Mitterrand advocated: "Whatever the problem, our answer is the same, more Europe."

The WEU admitted a host of new members in the mid 1990's. These included Greece and the non-EU, NATO member countries of Iceland, Norway, Turkey, Hungary, Poland, the Czech Republic, Austria, Finland, and Sweden. The European Council met in Cologne in June of 1999 and decided on a common policy on Russia which was the first use of the Common Foreign and Security Policy and adopted the declaration on Kosovo.

In relation to the European Security and Defense Policy, the Council declared that the EU must have the capacity for autonomous action, backed up by credible military forces, the means to decide to use them, and a readiness to do so, in order to respond to international crises without prejudice to actions by NATO." In 2000, the European Council at Nice established the decision making bodies (Political and Security Committee and a Military Committee reinforced by a Military Staff) and a crisis reaction force of sixty thousand soldiers.

In May of 2001, leading members of the EU's newly established military organizations, high-ranking officials and military personnel from the various Member States, and members of several European military and political think-tanks met in Berlin for a colloquy where they established the EU's security concepts and risks. Over four hundred participants from over thirty countries attended and all discussed security issues that would affect Europe and the EU's development of its own military. Professor de Wijk of the Royal Military Academy in Breda summed up the colloquy's purpose when he stated: At the same time, the US must accept the EU as an equal partner. We may have different views, but in the final analysis we share the same historical and cultural background and seek to protect the same values and interests. Moreover, only a military capable EU can help defend common EU-US interests.

Indeed, as the EU has global interests, the EU should develop capabilities with a truly global reach. I am very much against a division of labor where Europe sees to Europe and the USA sees to the rest of the world. For that reason, the security concept of the European Union must contain guidance for the development of power projection capabilities which can be deployed worldwide. In practice, a EU security concept should deal with the following questions: how to link the EU's military capabilities to its political objectives? Where and when the EU will make use of its military capabilities? What kind of operations will be conducted? How these operations will be conducted? What kind of military forces are required to conduct these operations?

Although the Amsterdam Treaty gave the WEU an integral role in giving the EU an independent defense capability, playing a major role in the Petersburg tasks in November 2000, WEU Ministers met in Marseille and agreed to begin transferring the organization's capabilities and functions to the European Union, under its developing Common Foreign and Security Policy (CFSP) and European Security and Defense Policy (ESDP).

In January 2002, the WEU's Security Studies Institute and the Satellite Centre transferred to the EU and became the European Union Institute for Security Studies and the European Union Satellite Centre. The Nice Treaty removed the role given to the WEU in the Amsterdam Treaty. The European Defense Agency is a continuation of the work of the Western European Armaments Organization (WEAO) and the Western European Armaments Group (WEAG). It represents the transference of their functions from the WEU and to the EU framework, and thus continues the decommissioning of the WEU.

The European Defense Agency (EDA) is an agency of the European Union headquartered in Brussels. Set up in July 2004, it is a Common Foreign and Security Policy (CFSP) body set which reports to the Council of the European Union.

The Lisbon Treaty scrapped the WEU and kept the mutual defense clause of the Treaty of Brussels as a basis for EU mutual defense arrangement. The Treaty of Lisbon states the following: "The common security and defense policy shall include the progressive framing of a common defense policy. This will lead to a common defense, when the European Council, acting unanimously, so decides."

In February of 2009, the European Parliament voted in favor of the creation of Synchronized Armed Forces Europe (SAFE) as a first step towards a true military force. An EU directorate will direct SAFE with training standards and operational doctrine. SAFE created an EU "Council of Defense Ministers" and a European statute for soldiers governing training standards, operational doctrine and freedom of operational action. SAFE is based on voluntary participation and will lead to the synchronization of the European forces. SAFE aims to develop an integrated European security structure. There will be civil and military capabilities in the member countries' reach.

According to the November 17, 2009, Times Online, Italy will push for the creation of a European Army after the adoption of the Lisbon Treaty. According to the article, Franco Frattini, the Italian Foreign Minister, said that the Lisbon Treaty established "that if some countries want to enter into reinforced co-operation between themselves they can do so." This agreement existed with the euro and the Schengen accords on frontier-free travel, and a "common European defense" will take the same approach. Mr. Frattini suggested that if there was a European army one nation can send planes, another tanks and another armored cars. He said this is the idea of a European army.

The EU's army continues to evolve and will evolve into the eventual powerful military the Scripture's forecast. The Lisbon Treaty added the necessary foundation for the EU's military evolution.

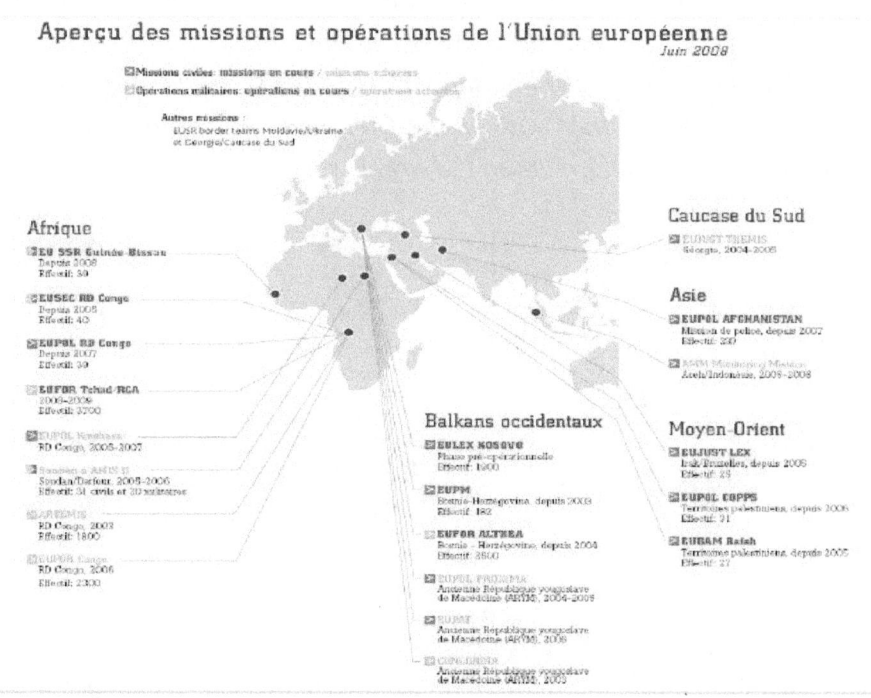

MEDIA INSIGHT (MACLEANS.CA)
KATIE ENGELHART: NOW IS THE TIME TO MOUNT A EUROPEAN ARMY, LEADERS CONCLUDE

"Later this year, the leaders of European Union nations will meet in Brussels for their annual European council. On the agenda: a discussion of Europe's military might. At the summit, it's likely that two equally bold visions for European defense will be put forward. One would see the union's 27 member states pool military resources as never before-with an eye to eventually building a bona fide EU army. ...In London, it is talk of a potential pullout from the EU that dominates. But elsewhere, calls for a pan-European military are growing-with France and Germany leading the charge. In September, a group of EU foreign ministers spelled it out directly, weighing, in a controversial report, the possibility of a European army...Today, supporters of the still-elusive EU army insist that pooling military might is the only way for the Continent to keep its fists up. ...And they argue there are already precursors to an EU army.

10

THE EU AND THE NATIONS OF THE WORLD

The common market is having such a colossal effect on the continent of Europe that all European 20 nations want some form of associate status with the European Union. Even Russia expressed a desire to join. The Union is forming association agreements with the remaining European nations that do not hold EU membership. These nations will enact common market legislation. Some have linked their currencies to the ECU without having any say in EU laws. As this occurs, the EU's sphere of influence broadens beyond its existing members. The EU is like a giant octopus; its long tentacles reach into the rest of Europe and beyond.

European leaders established the EFTA, or European Free Trade Association, whose members included Austria, Finland, Iceland, Norway, Sweden, and Switzerland, in 1959. In 1984, the Luxembourg Declaration created a free trade area embracing the eighteen nations of both the EU and the EFTA. In 1990, the EFTA and EU foreign ministers opened formal negotiations to create a "European Economic Space," where goods, services, capital, and people would flow freely between the countries of both groupings. The EEA represented the world's biggest free trade area, with 380 million consumers. It accounts for 46 percent of world trade. In 1994, European leaders established the European Economic Area. It allows the EFTA countries to participate in the European single market without joining the EU. Since Austria, Finland and Sweden jointed the EU in 1995, Iceland, Liechtenstein and Norway are its remaining members.

On May 7, 2009 the EU inaugurated in Prague the Eastern Partnership. It provides an institutionalized forum for discussing visa agreements, free trade deals and strategic partnership agreements with the EU's eastern neighbors. Controlled directly by the EU Commission, its geographical scope consists of Belarus, Armenia, Azerbaijan, Georgia, Moldova and Ukraine. Russia accused the EU of trying to carve out a new sphere of influence. An EU official retorted by stating: "We're responding to the demands of these countries, and the economic reality is that most of their trade is done with the EU." The EU negotiated these various pacts to increase its stature and position in the world. According to Stanley

Hoffman, Chairman of the Center of European Studies at Harvard: "Clearly the purpose of the whole effort is not merely to increase wealth by removing obstacles to production and technological progress, but also to increase Europe's power in a world in which economic and financial clout is as important as military might."

In addition, as EU legislation extends into these countries, they will come under the EU's sphere of influence. They will have to adopt EU laws without any voice in EU government. The Antichrist will easily institute his political policies throughout these nations. The EEA exists as a regional grouping of nations in a common pact. With the fall of the Berlin Wall, Eastern European countries voiced their desire to join the EU. This event marked the beginning of a political identity for the European Union. Eastern Europe looked to the EU for aid and investment, as opposed to looking towards the US and they wanted associate status with the EU which they more than obtained.

The Euro-Mediterranean Free Trade Area (EMFTA) is a free trade zone still evolving based on the Barcelona Declaration, a framework plan adopted in 1995 through association agreements between Brussels and each state bordering the Mediterranean. The countries participating include Algeria, Egypt, Israel, Jordan, Lebanon, Morocco, Syria, Turkey, Tunisia and the Palestinian Authority. The agreement involves trade, investment, and deep political reform which Brussels calls "approximation" of other countries' legal and political institutions with its own. The aim is a "genuine free trade area as soon as possible." The fall of Communism ushered in a New World Order, and thereby paved the way for the revival of the Roman Empire and the fulfillment of the prophecies for the "latter days." An EU report on Eastern Europe in 1991 affirmed: "The map is being redrawn with the Community firmly at the heart of the new Europe. This Europe is to emerge as a new force in the balance of world power, a fact already recognized by the US of America, Japan, and the Soviet Union.

THE REVIVED ROMAN EMPIRE

The EU bears many similarities to the Old Roman Empire. European Union leaders such as Former Belgian Prime Minister and candidate for Presidency of the EU Commission, Guy Verhofstadt classify the Union as an Empire.

In September 2007, a reporter asked Commission President Jose Manuel Barroso what type of political entity the Union will be after the Lisbon Treaty is enforced. Barroso responded that the European Union will not be a superstate, that it is a unique organization of free countries that are united, that started to work together in cooperation. He said that the national level is not enough for today's problems such as climate change. "We are not forming a superstate, there is not such a risk, on the contrary what we are seeing is the formation of something different. The rationale for the reform is keeping the great vision of the founding fathers."

He then called the EU "an unidentified political object, a very successful experiment. In the history of institutions' we never had such a thing. Sometimes I like to compare the European Union to the creation of empires, because we have the dimension of empires, but there is a great difference from the empires that were created through force, we are the first non-imperial empire, we have 27 countries that decided to work together and pool their sovereignty." Geographically, the EU lies within the Roman Empire's old borders. The Roman Empire had its own currency and army. It used two languages for everyday communication: Latin and Greek. In the same way, the European Union recognizes French and English. The Roman Empire built roads throughout the whole of its empire. The Channel Tunnel, which links Britain to the rest of the continent, is "the first truly integrated pan-European transport system since the Roman roads."

The EU's has its own national anthem, which coincidentally is Beethoven's "Ode to Joy," and the melody for the Christian hymn "Faithful, Faithful We Adore Thee." The EU has a motto, "united in diversity," and even its own holidays. EU citizens celebrate May 9 as Shuman Day the date that marked the birth of the EU in the same way Americans celebrate the 4th of July. The EU's flag mentioned earlier which is a circle of twelve stars on a blue background, depicts Judeo- Christian symbolism. The stars symbolize the twelve tribes of Israel and the twelve apostles, along with the twelve months in a year, and the Greek myth that speaks of the twelve labors Hercules performed to gain immortality.

THE EU CAPITAL

Some Bible scholars believe that Rome will become the headquarters of the final world empire. Although Rome is the city where the EU was established, and was the location of the conference on political union, it is not the capital of the new Europe. The capital is Brussels, Belgium, headquarters of the European Commission. Luxembourg is the financial and legal capital of the Union. The European Parliament meets in Strasbourg, France. Around the time of Christ, Belgium lay just within the Roman Empire's northern border. It divided the conquered territory from the unconquered Germanic and Russian lands. In modern times, Brussels is centrally located between the EU, and eastern bloc nations. During the first advent of Christ, the world's population lived primarily around the Middle East and Mediterranean regions, and Rome was central to the Empire. The final world empire will have a sphere of influence over many more nations.

The Antichrist's headquarters change after the middle of the Tribulation. Daniel 11:45 attests: "and he shall plant the tabernacles of his palace between the seas in the glorious holy mountain; yet he shall come to his end, and none shall help him." Near the time of the end, the Antichrist will move his headquarters to Jerusalem, which, besides being the Holy City, is more central to the world at large. The Antichrist will, at this time, be in control of the Middle East region.

Revelation 13:2 tells us that the Dragon gives Antichrist "his power, his throne, and great authority." The European Union is evolving into a world power that will act as the launching pad for the devices of Satan. The Antichrist's reign here on earth will mimic that of Jesus Christ. While society grows more in line with Christ's warnings and natural disasters increase, the European Union evolves into the final world empire. Former US Senate Majority leader George Mitchell called "the economic integration of Western Europe the most important event of our times." The idea of reuniting Europe has existed since the fall of the Roman Empire. The formation of the European Union will end up becoming the single most important attempt in world history.

The Scriptures specifically state that the Antichrist will raise the Community to its pinnacle of power. The Union will not be as powerful at the time of his appointment. From the signing of the treaty, the Antichrist will have three years to bring the Union to its height of power. This does not include his efforts before the start of the Tribulation. The lust for power that presently exists among Unionists provides the Antichrist with an opportune climate to pursue his demoniac ambitions.

11

THE THRONES OF EUROPE

The European Court of Justice (ECJ) has risen from relative obscurity to become an important and influential aspect of the European Union. Together with the General Court (previously known as the Court of First Instance), the ECJ is responsible for ensuring uniform interpretation of EU treaties. Despite its relative unobtrusiveness compared to other EU institutions, the ECJ has become increasingly powerful and wields considerably more authority than many other international courts. The Court has been active in extending the reach of Community law by constitutionalizing the treaties; extending the remit of the law and using its power to propagate further European integration

THE EUROPEAN HIERARCHY

And he shall speak great words against the most High, and shall wear out the saints of the most High, and think to change times and laws: and they shall be given into his hand until a time and times and the dividing of time (Daniel 7:25).

THE TEN HORN FEDERATON

"We do not want another committee. We have too many already. What we want is a man of sufficient stature to head the allegiance of all people and to lift us out of the economic morass in which we are sinking. Send us such a man and be he god or the Devil we will receive him," Former Belgian Prime Minister, lst President of the ED Parliament: Paul-Henri Spaak. Daniel's visions of the final world empire, describe a distinct political government, and provide a view to its institutional and structural make-up. Under the Antichrist's authority, it reaches its zenith of power. Daniel describes it as "dreadful and terrible and exceedingly strong." The Beast devours and breaks in pieces its enemies to the point of crushing their remains (Dan. 7:7). John likewise sees it in its final form "rising up out of the sea"-a figurative illustration of its rise to power (Rev. 13:1). This political power possesses the combined strength of all the empires before it. Unlike them, it devours and treads down the entire earth (Dan. 7:23, Rev. 13:2).

The Beast has ten horns, and among them comes up a little horn who is the Antichrist (Dan. 7:7-8). Daniel 7:24 states that "the ten horns are ten kings who shall arise from this kingdom: and another shall rise after them." Revelation 13:1 depicts the horns as wearing crowns. Both, the book of Daniel and the Revelation identify the horns as kings (Rev. 17:12). The prophets add that these kingdoms do not in exist at the time of the writings. European nations did not come into being until over a millennium later. Only in this last couple of centuries have these nations reigned as separate, sovereign kingdoms. The horns wearing crowns signify established kingdoms or nations. The little horn appears after the kings, and "comes up" among them. His small horn represents a relatively new political seat on the world stage when he takes power. Horns grow with age, but this one grows extremely large, quickly. Daniel tells us, "And out of one of them came a little horn, which grew exceedingly great, toward the south, toward the east, and toward the glorious land" (Dan. 8:9-10).

Despite the EU's newness in the international arena, it has the potential to create a dictatorship that could obtain world rule. Satan himself provides the Antichrist with a political position by which he rises to greatness and conquers the world. He wears no crown because he is not the king of any one nation, yet he leads the federation. The Antichrist exists in a symbiotic relationship with the kings. Revelation 17:13 tells us: "These are of one mind and they will give their power and authority to the beast."

The Antichrist partners with the Kings. Some label the Union a confederation. The Union considers itself a federation. In a confederation, nations or states share governmental tasks. In a federation, the members relinquish some of their sovereignty to a higher authority, which makes the laws and regulations for the signing states. The Scriptures describe the federation's members as actual nations, not provinces or states. The Bible's federation acts as a dictatorship.

THE TREATY OF ROME

Seven main institutions (based on the Treaty of Rome) make up the European Union: the Commission, the European Parliament, the Council of Ministers, the Court of Justice, and the Court of Auditors. Nine additional treaties amended the Treaty of Rome, which established the European Union on March 1, 1957. The recent Lisbon Treaty added two more institutions: the European Central Bank, and the Council of Europe which the EU previously regarded as governing bodies but not official institutions. The Treaties provide the format for the EU's institutional structure and the agreements by which the signing nations are to abide. The member nations surrender parts of their national sovereignty to the higher authority.

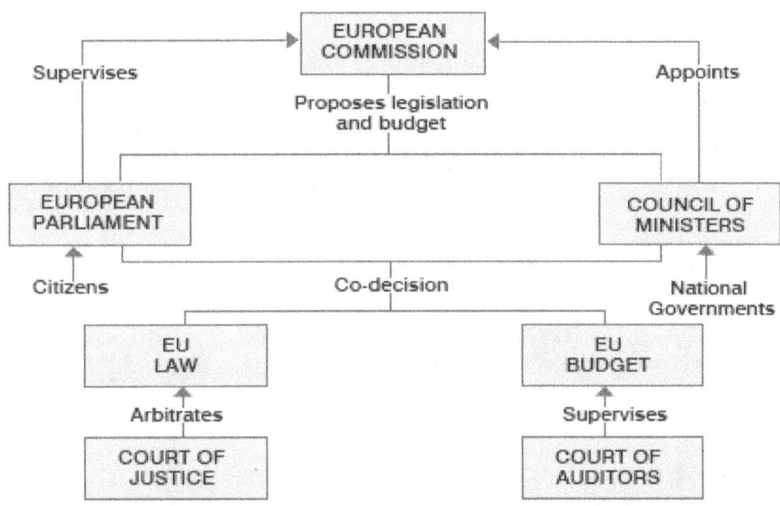

THE COUNCIL OF THE EUROPEAN UNION

The Antichrist will be in a federation with ten kings. These kings are the Council of The European Union formerly named the Council of Ministers. They are the governmental heads of each of the Member States. Each nation addresses them by a different title, but the Bible refers to them as kings. "Prime ministers" and "presidents" have essentially the same meaning. The Council represents the highest decision-making authority in the EU, and holds the preeminent position in the institutional power balance. Although the Council does not initiate EU laws, it must approve all Community legislation. Its secretariat is located in Brussels. The Council also concludes, on behalf of the EU, all international agreements; makes the decisions necessary for framing and implementing the Common

Foreign and Security Policy; and adopts measures in the field of police and judicial cooperation.

The Bible always refers to the word "council" in a negative context. In Mark 13:9, Christ warns the Jews during the Tribulation to "watch out for yourselves: for they will deliver you up to councils; and you will be beaten in the synagogues. And you will be brought before rulers and kings for My sake, for a testimony to them." The EU's Council of Ministers may be one of the councils Christ mentioned in Scripture. The scriptures specifically mention councils and two councils exist within the EU's institutional structure.

It is common knowledge among journalists covering the EU that the Council of Ministers meets in secret. The Belmont European Policy Center stated, in a report on the Maastricht Treaty, that the "EC Council of Ministers remains the most secretive of Community institutions." On this subject, The Economist commented that the ministers are "The EC's real legislature and the only one in the world that does not let in the public."

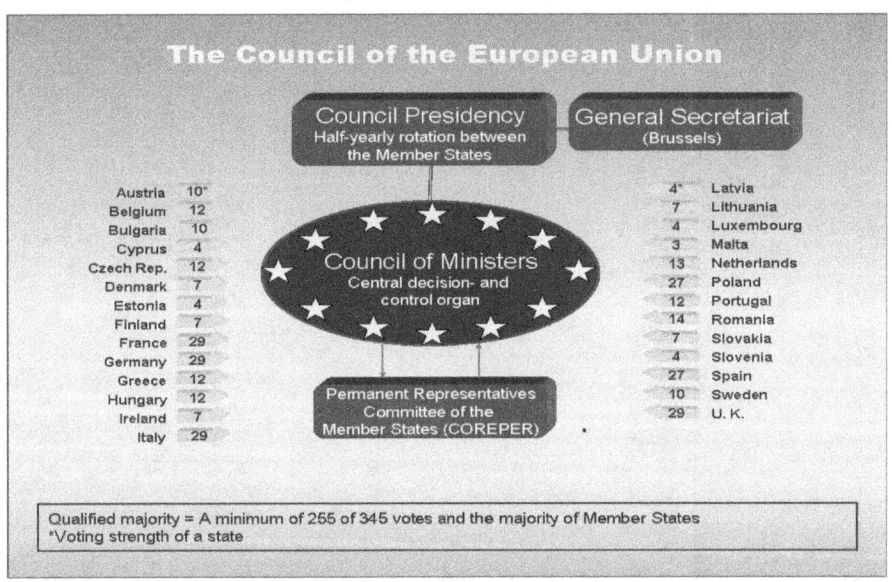

In 2009 when EU leaders met to nominate the first president of the Council and foreign affairs minister, the Former Lavian president Vaira Vike-Freiberga, said that EU leaders conducted the nomination process with Soviet-style secrecy and contempt for the public. He attacked the EU for operating in "darkness and behind closed doors" and said it should "stop working like the former Soviet Union." The Council of Ministers already acts in an undemocratic fashion. The previous chapter discussed the ambition that reigns among these leaders for leading superpower status which creates the climate for a powerful leader. Revelation 17:12 describes the ten horns as ten kings who "receive authority for one hour as kings with the beast." During the Tribulation, the Council promotes the Antichrist's agenda and essentially acts in a marriage type of relationship with him. They act together as if joined with the Antichrist leading. As Jesus led his disciples, the Antichrist will lead the Prime Ministers or Presidents.

THE EU COMMISSION: THE SEAT OF THE ANTICHRIST

When the European member nations signed the Treaty of Rome, they agreed to hand over some of their powers to a higher authority called the Commission. As the EU's executive arm, it acts as an overseer of the EU Treaties, and upholds them. Members of the Commission represent the interests of the Union as a whole. The size of its staff is comparable to the US Department of Commerce.

The Commission, a non-elected body, is comprised of representatives from each of the member nations. The Commission has a president who sits among the Council of the European Union (or "kings"). He is responsible for the major decisions and laws that move the EU forward into the international arena as a single political and economic entity. Former Belgian Prime Minister Guy Verhofstadt suggested changing its name to the "European Government", calling the present name of Commission: "ridiculous" because of its governmental powers. Coincidentally, the Commission's headquarters are located in Brussels with the President's office and the Commission's meeting room based on the 13th floor of the Berlaymont building.

The Commission President's position fits the description of the "little horn" in Daniel for he stands among the ten horns or prime ministers and unlike the kings which head nations, he has no nation beneath him, he heads the federation. The horn signifies a relatively new position on the world stage which fits the EU Commission. The Scriptures provide specific details concerning the Antichrist's authorities. The political seat he holds must allow him the powers cited in the prophetic writings.

THE EU COMMISSON PRESIDENCY PROVIDES THE ANTICHRIST WITH THE POWERS OUTLINED IN SCRIPTURE-HIS POSITION MUST ALLOW HIM A MINIMUM OF A SEVEN-YEAR TERM

Daniel 9:27 states: "Then he shall confirm a covenant with many for one week," i.e., seven years. The seven-year Tribulation begins with the signing of a peace treaty with Israel. The Antichrist is in power before the Tribulation begins. No leader signs a treaty on the day of his election. The Council of Ministers appoints the Commission President to a five-year renewable term. They make these appointments in years ending in four and nine.

MEDIA INSIGHT (PRESSEUROPE.EU)

COUNTRIES FOR A UNITED STATES OF EUROPE

Ten EU foreign ministers participating in a "study group for the future of Europe" aim to exert pressure to transform the EU into a federation along the lines of the US. Together they have prepared what the front-page headline in Die Presse describes as a "Plan for transformation into a European state."

The "study group for the future" ... proposes to put an end to the dominance of national government leaders and give greater authority to the European Commission - in particular the European Commission president...

THE VICE PRESIDENT OF THE COMMISSION

The Lisbon Treaty created the position called High Representative of the Union for Foreign Affairs and Security Policy which in actuality will serve as the European Union's Foreign Minister. The Former position of High Representative merged with the European Commissioner for External Relations to produce the new Foreign Minister position. The rejected Constitution called the position, Union Minister for Foreign Affairs. The Minister would also be a Vice-President in the Commission.

THE EUROPEAN PARLIAMENT

The Parliament directly represents the people of Europe and links to the toes on the image in the book of Daniel. As with all other EU institutions, the EU parliament has evolved since its inception. In 1974, the Heads of Government agreed to permit direct elections. In 1979, the EU held the first direct elections. Although the EU Parliament is the second largest democratic electorate in the world, second to India, but unlike most national parliaments, the EU parliament does not have legislative initiative. The Parliament's 736 members, elected every five years by voters in all Member States, have significant power over budgetary matters. They scrutinize, draft EU legislation, question the Commission and Council of Ministers on their conduct of EU affairs, and debate topical issues.

Acting as a check upon the Commission, Article 140 of the Treaty of Rome requires Commissioners to appear before Parliament to respond to questions. The Commission submits an annual report of its activities to the Parliament. The Commission is required to resign as a body if the Parliament adopts a motion of censure against it. Of the four attempted motions of censure, none succeeded.

A majority of Parliament must approve international treaties-save certain trade agreements. In many other areas the Parliament may amend laws, unless the European Commission and all members of the Council object.

The Parliament may ask the Commission to propose laws, and may challenge acts of the Commission or Council in the Court of Justice. The Council must consult the Parliament on who heads the Commission, and must approve the choice of a new team of Commissioners. The EU Parliament compares to the US Congress with its President, which the people elect for two and a half year terms acting as its speaker.

Some end time watchers reported on the European Parliament Presidency as the possible launching pad for the Antichrist, assuming this President led the Union. The Union's institutional structure comprises of five presidents: the Council's, Parliaments, Court of Justice's, Court of Auditors and the Commission. Of the five, the Commission President heads the European Union.

THE EUROPEAN COURT OF JUSTICE

The Court of Justice, located in Luxembourg, is comprised of 27 judges, one from each member state plus one other, assisted by 8 advocates-general. The Council of the European Union appoints the judges and advocates-general for six-year renewable terms. The judges elect the President of the Court of Justice for a renewable term of three years.

The President presides over hearings and deliberations, directing both judicial business and administration. The EU's Court parallels the US Supreme Court. It enforces EU treaties, determines the interpretation and implementation of Union legislation, and resolves conflicts between Union and national laws. Basically it makes sure that the Member States effectively apply the laws. Union law (based on the Treaties of Rome) and national law of the individual member countries now intertwine. Its decisions attracts more and more of the national courts' attention. Court decisions strengthen EU institutions and promote EU policies. Verdicts reached by simple majority are binding on all parties, and are not subject to appeal.

THE EUROPEAN COURT OF AUDITORS

The Maastricht Treaty established the Court of Auditors as the fifth institution of the EU. The Court of Auditors examines the accounts of all of the Union's revenues and expenditures. One member from each EU member state and a President, make up the Court. The Court has no judicial functions. It is rather a professional external investigatory audit agency.

 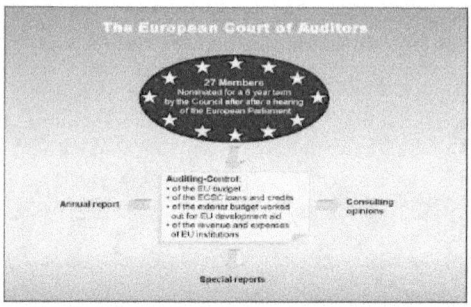

The Court checks if officials implement the budget of the European Union correctly, and ensures that EU funds are spent legally and with sound management. A staff of approximately 800 auditors, translators and administrators supports the Court.

THE EUROPEAN COUNCIL

The European Councils held their first meeting in 1961 and formalized them after 1974. These brought together the Commission President and the leaders of the EU countries in deciding political guidelines for the Union. The Council has no formal executive or legislative powers; it deals with major issues and meets about four times a year in Brussels.

The Lisbon Treaty made the European Council a full-fledged European institution. It is headed by a President. Elected by the Council for two and a half years; the President prepares the Council's work, ensures its continuity and works to secure consensus among member countries. The position is a non-executive, administrative role. The highest political body of the EU, it is chaired by a member of the Council of the European Union formerly known as the Council of Ministers President. He can call meetings beyond the four that are formally required to take place. Lisbon gave the Council greater say over a variety of EU related matters. While the Commission and Council of the European Union are two separate institutions that work together, the European Council brings these two groups together as one institution.

THE EUROPEAN CENTRAL BANK

Established in 1998 and modeled on the German Bundesbank, the bank which was once independent from any European or national institution is now a governmental institution of the European Union. The Governing Council, the supreme decision making body of the European Central Bank (ECB) takes decisions on monetary policy, interest rates and reserves of the ESCB along with other matters. The Union only allows the President of the European Council, the President of the EU Commission and members to attend its meetings. Governing Council members represent the interests of the Eurozone as a whole.

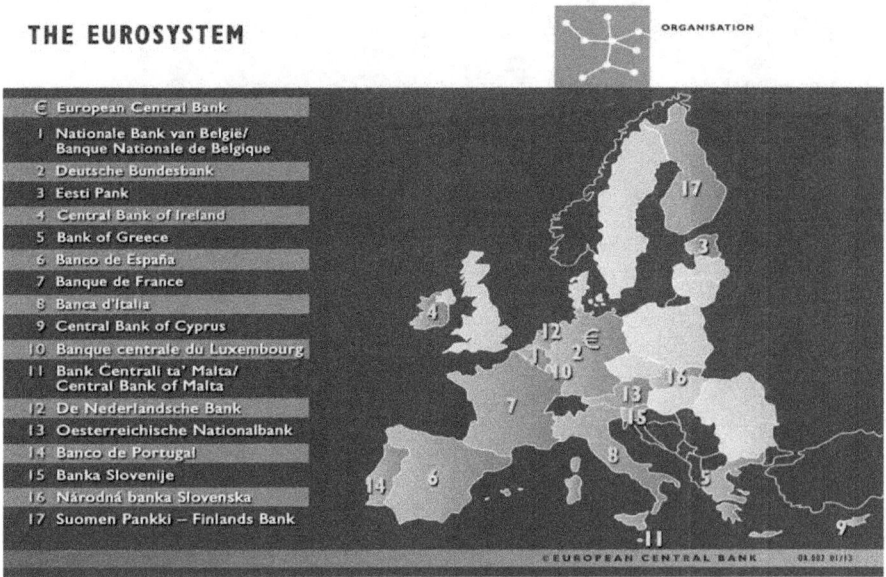

The Economic and Social Committee represents the views and interests of EU nationals. The Committee of the Regions ensures the respect of regional and local identities and prerogatives. In addition the EU has other bodies that play specialized roles, the European Investment bank, European Investment Fund, European Ombudsman, European Data Protection Supervisor, Office for Official Publications of the European Communities, European Personnel Selection Office and the European Administrative School.

12

THE ANTICHRIST

He will emerge from obscurity, but by dint of his diplomatic skill he will win the admiration and compel the cooperation of the political world. In the early stages of his career he appears as "a little horn" (or power), but it is not long before he climbs the ladder of fame, and by means of brilliant statesmanship, ascends its topmost rung. Like the majority of politicians, he will not scruple to employ questionable methods; in fact it will be by diplomatic chicanery and intrigue that he will win his early successes. Daniel 11:21 tells us that at first they will not give to him the honor of the kingdom, but "he shall come in peaceably, and obtain the kingdom by flatteries." Once he gains the ascendancy none will dare to challenge his authority. Kings will be his pawns and princes his playthings.

THE CHARACTERISTICS OF THE ANTICHRIST

HE WILL BECOME STRONG WITH A SMALL NUMBER OF PEOPLE

Daniel 11:21, 23, states: "And in his place shall arise a vile person, to whom they will not give the honor of royalty; but he shall come in peaceably and seize the kingdom by intrigue. And after the league is made with him he shall act deceitfully; for he shall come up and become strong with a small number of people."

Some say these passages refer to Antiochus IV Epiphanes, a ruler of ancient Greece, reputed as a famous persecutor of the Jews. While he represents a prototype of the final world ruler; this prediction describes how the Antichrist comes into power. The people do not elect the Commission President. The Council of Ministers consults with the European Parliament, and nominates the person they intend to appoint to the Commission presidency. This nomination, subject to a vote and the approval of the European Parliament, concludes by the Council of Ministers' appointment. The "small number of people" refers to this close-knit group of EU bureaucrats who place him in power. It may also signify his being a prime minister from one of the smaller EU countries. To date, European Commission Presidents have held prior EU posts such as officials from one of the Member States and former prime ministers.

During the 2009 nomination of the first EU Council President, journalists noted that EU leaders strategized picking someone from a small country with little international power instead of a charismatic heavyweight. As the EU chose former Belgian Prime Minister Herman van Rompuy as the new Council President and Britain's Catherine Ashton for the post of EU High Representative a headline reported, "Unknown duo chosen as new faces of Europe." The idea is that a low key leader will be more effective in achieving consensus among so many leaders of the various nations than a well-known charismatic one. According to the Associated Press: "for EU leaders to pick a boss they can all live with, they must strike the right balance between big countries and small, east and west, socialists and conservatives, perhaps male and female. They must maneuver between proponents of a strong Europe and those who fear it-Eurocentric's and euro skeptics, in the local parlance." The EU will select the leader who the Bible deems as the Antichrist in the same manner.

HE WILL BE IN A FEDERATON WITH TEN KINGS

Revelation 17:12-13 tells us: "And the ten horns which you saw are ten kings who have received no kingdom as yet; but they receive authority for one hour as kings with the beast, these are of one mind, and they will give their power and authority to the beast."

This verse describes the relationship of the ten kings to the Antichrist. They both strive for the same goals. One entity does not exist without the other. The Council of The European (formerly Council of Ministers) give their strength and power to the Commission. Without the member nations that hand over their authority to the Commission, there would be no European Union. Several articles in the EU Treaty reflect their having one mind. Article 162 states: "The Council and the Commission shall consult each other and settle by common accord their methods of cooperation."

The Scriptures are unprecedented in their accuracy and detail. Although written 1,900 years ago, one Bible verse epitomizes the contents of two treaties in just 14 words.

"These shall have one mind and shall give their power and strength unto the Beast."

Over and over, one reads of the Commission's and Council Ministers' simultaneous role. Peter Ludlow, the founding director of the Centre For European Policy Studies think-tank in Brussels, referred to the

Commission-Council relationship as a "partnership." Of the EU's institutions, the Commission and the Council (of Ministers) represent the leading authorities. The Court enforces EU laws, and the Parliament acts as a forum with some legislative powers.

HE WILL BE BOTH PRESIDENT AND FOREIGN MINISTER

The Commission negotiates treaties, making agreements with other nations and with world organizations. It makes recommendations to the Council of the European Union i.e. the Council of Ministers, which authorizes the opening of negotiations and conducts them. Special committees formed by the Council assist the Commission. The Commission proposes agreements to the Council, which votes by a qualified majority, consults with the European Parliament, and then concludes the agreements. The Commission President thus negotiates and signs treaties with other nations. The Commission can impose sanctions on third world countries. It maintains EU relations with the UN, WTO and all other world institutions. The Council and the Commission take responsibility for ensuring the consistency of all EU policies.

THE ANTICHRIST WILL HAVE A DIVERSE ROLE FROM THAT OF THE TEN KINGS

Daniel 7:24 states: "The ten horns are ten kings who shall arise; from this kingdom and another shall rise after them; he shall be different from the first ones."

As the EU's executive arm, the Commission's major responsibility is to oversee EU treaties. It initiates EU laws and policy. Thus, the Higher Authority acts as the lawmaker while the Council of the European Union approves the laws.

HIS POSITION WILL GIVE HIM THE POWER TO EXPEL THREE OF THE KINGS

Daniel 7:24 continues, "…and shall subdue three kings." Regarded as the "Guardian of the Treaties," the Commission can take action against member governments that it believes have violated their treaty obligations. It proposes to the Court of Justice the fines imposed on Member States proven in default under the treaty. Presently, the Union cannot expel a Member, but allowing this action has come under discussion. The Lisbon Treaty amended articles to allow a nation to withdraw from the Union.

AUTHORITY TO DETERMINE WHO WILL BUY AND SELL WITH HIS GOVERNMENT

Revelation 13:17 tells us: "and that no one may buy or sell, except one who has the mark, or the name of the beast, or the number of his name."

This passage deals with individuals living under the Antichrist's dictatorship, and extends to persons worldwide. The Commission initiates the Union's internal market policy and external trade, including that with the US. It determines the guidelines for trade with other countries, as well as for its members within the Union. Thus, the Commission determines with whom it will buy and sell, and how. The Commission also negotiates international trade agreements.

THE ANTICHRIST WILL CHANGE TIMES AND LAWS

Daniel 7:25 reports: "He shall speak pompous words against the Most High, shall persecute the saints of the Most High, and shall intend to change times and laws." The Commission introduces EU legislation, carries out decisions, and oversees the enforcement of European laws. With this authority, the Antichrist can easily implement his laws and change existing ones.

HE WILL HAVE DIRECT ACCESS TO RECENT TECHNOLOGICAL ACHIEVEMENTS, AND CONTROL OVER THE DEVELOPMENT OF NEW TECHNOLOGIES

Revelation 13:16-17 states: "And he causes all, both small and great, rich and poor, free and slave, to receive a mark on their foreheads; And that no one may buy or sell, except one who has the mark, or the name of the beast, or the number of his name." The Commission oversees the research and development of new technologies. It determines which programs and projects will receive funding. The development of new technologies remains an EU priority. The Antichrist will have access to those new technological systems, and the power to authorize their implementation.

HIS GOVERNMENT MUST GIVE RISE TO A DICTATORSHIP

Revelation 13:15 tells us that he was granted power to give breath to the image of the beast, that the image of the beast should both speak, and cause that as many as would not worship the image of the beast to be killed." The Antichrist kills those who do not worship him-a common trait of most dictatorships. Dictators reign from political positions that provide them with complete authority. The Commission's authorities are not balanced by either the Court of Justice or the Parliament. The European people do not elect its members, although it is the EU's executive arm, making it a non-democratic institution.

Former British Prime Minister Margaret Thatcher, in a major speech in Bruges, Belgium, assailed the idea of a supranational European State. In an address to the European Parliament in Strasbourg, France,

Jacques Delors had predicted that by the mid-1990s, the EU would develop "an embryo European government." Thatcher referred to these possible developments as "a nightmare" that would create "bureaucratic centralism" in the EU. She also warned:

"We fought two world wars to make the world a safer place for democracy. Here we are preaching more democracy to the old Communist Soviet Union and ourselves practicing less democracy and more bureaucracy."

During Thatcher's tenure as Prime Minister, she stood as a strong opponent of a federal Europe and represented the lone ranger among the other members of the European Council. In her later years she gave speeches against a European superstate. Mrs. Thatcher stated that a United States of Europe will endanger world peace. Thatcher uttered her strongest statement when she called the European Federalist project, "a nightmare." She asked: "Were it to come about does anyone suppose that such a power would not soon become a rival to America? ......If this new Europe were not to follow the path to separate great power status, it would be the first such power in history to renounce its independent role."

Margaret Thatcher saw from the beginning that the Commission held too much power in the institutional power balance. She understood that this amount of centralized power can lead to a dictatorship. While she never directly stated these words she used other lighter terms which place the Union's structure in a similar sphere. Maurie Duverger commented in L'Express of Paris, reprinted in World Press Review, that: After 1992, nearly 80 percent of economic regulations will be enacted by the EU in Brussels, not in the capitals of the Member States. That means that decisions will be taken away from parliaments elected by universal suffrage and handed over to a political system that will largely escape the grasp of such parliaments. Europe invented democracy. But the more Europe unites, the more democracy is whittled away. As national powers are gradually reduced by the growth of a supra-national power, citizens will be chagrined. Former EU European Parliamentarian David Martin, commenting on the EU's "democratic deficit" and need for institutional reform, stated: "If the EC was a state and applied to join the Community, it would be turned down on the grounds that it was not a democracy."

Tony Benn, one of the most prominent figures in postwar British politics, and a longtime Labor Party member, affirmed: "The European Community is entirely undemocratic. It is run largely by commissioners who are not elected and cannot be removed. The Council of Ministers is the only legislative body in what's called the 'free world' that meets in secret." Secretiveness is a common characteristic of dictatorships. Certain EU legislation is fashioned in a secretive, undemocratic fashion. The Belmont European Policy Center stated that: "Unfortunately, the EU Treaty contains certain provisions, which govern Co-decision Procedure...having the effect of making the legislative processes unnecessarily secretive and prima facie inconsistent with the principles of democratic government." This report emphasized the secretiveness of Council of Ministers meetings, which echoes throughout several foreign affairs journals and articles.

The Antichrist's federation will have secret agendas. Amazingly, when the Antichrist takes his position as President of the European Union Commission, he will have the platform for his dictatorship. Of all the Institutions, the Commission holds the greatest powers, and the other EU governmental bodies do not balance its authorities. The former journal European Affairs stated: "At present the European institutions are upside down. The only institution with democratic legitimacy on a European scale, the European Parliament, has consultative powers only. The most dynamic body, the one that has the power to get things moving, is arbitrarily appointed and accountable to only one: the Commission of the European Communities."

The American Free Press upon Estonia's admission into the EU quoted former Estonian Prime Minister Edgar Savisaar, and others as comparing the EU with the Soviet Union. "The forced propaganda of the European Union is reminiscent of the Soviet Union's methods and brainwashing," Rolf Parve, wrote in Kesknadal, the weekly paper of the Center Party. "Moscow and Brussels differ in one point," Professor Igor Grazin, one of the leading anti-EU voices in Estonia says: "The Soviet Union theoretically allowed nations to leave the union. Brussels is creating organs, however, which would kill that idea in the bud." Savissar compared the "big bureaucratic system" of the EU with that of the Soviet Union. Currently, the EU is regarded by several politicians as a superstate, and they state this derogatorily.

According to Wikipedia: "a superstate is an agglomeration of nations and or/states, often linguistically and ethnically diverse under a single political-administrative structure. This is distinct from the concept of superpower, although these are frequently seen together. It is also distinct from the concept of empire where one nation dominates other nations through military, political, and economic power, as in the Roman Empire, although and empire may also be a superstate, as in ancient Persia, India and China.

HIS KINGDOM WILL BE DIVIDED AND WILL INVOLVE MANY MEN

Nebuchadnezzar's vision in Daniel 2:28-45 illustrates the Beast's complexity. The Bible states that the fourth kingdom is "strong as iron," and "breaks in pieces and shatters all things," Daniel adds that there is weakness amidst its strength. Daniel 2: 41-43 records: "Whereas you saw the feet and toes, partly of potter's clay and partly of iron, the kingdom shall be divided; yet the strength of the iron shall be in it, just as you saw the iron mixed with ceramic clay. And as the toes of the feet were partly of iron and partly of clay, so the kingdom shall be partly strong and partly fragile. As you saw iron mixed with ceramic clay, they will mingle with the seed of men; but they will not adhere to one another, just as iron does not mix with clay."

The iron and clay which makes up the image's toes do not mix. The iron legs have power to break in pieces and crush all that opposes the Beast. The Bible states that clay represents the seed of men. The potter's clay signifies a divided kingdom and the complexity within this kingdom-iron is firm, clay is brittle. The kingdom divides at the legs into feet and toes mingled with clay. John F. Walvoord, in his book Daniel: The Key to Prophetic Revelation, discusses this passage and relates the various interpretations from well known Bible expositors. A. C. Gaebelein states that "monarchies and clay represent democratic rule.' Lutheran Hebrew Old Testament scholar Johann Karl Friedrich Keil argues that "it is all the means employed by rulers to combine the different nationalities, a sort of intermarriage.' Walvoord concludes that this diversity, "whether this refers to race, political idealism or sectional interests,…will prevent the final form of the kingdom from having any real unity.'

The vision depicts an analogy of the European Union's institutional structure as it exists today. One iron leg represents the EU Commission, while the toes symbolize the Council of Ministers. The toes mingled with clay represent the sovereign nations who still hold elections and rule their countries while handing over specific powers to the EU Commission. Clay, or the democratic electoral process, conflicts with totalitarian rule. The Scriptures stand unprecedented in their accuracy. One must pay tribute to those Bible scholars who successfully interpreted prophetic passages while there no telltale signs in world affairs manifested. Some Bible Eschatologists teach that the Beast has ten toes which represent the ten nations because the Scripture refers to the feet of the image and feet have five toes a piece thus ten toes. The Scripture does not specify the number of toes which can be many. Dwight Pentecost sited Kelly's observation who that:

"There will be, before the age closes, the most remarkable union of two apparently contradictory conditions-a universal head of empire, a separate independent kingdom besides, each of which will have its own king; but that one man will be emperor over all these kings... God has said they shall be divided.…In virtue of the iron there will be a universal monarchy, while in virtue of the clay there will be separate kingdoms."

Europa the EU's website elaborates by stating about the EU's institutions: "The European Union (EU) is not a federation like the United States. Nor is it simply an organization for co-operation between governments, Like the United Nations. It is, in fact, unique. The countries that make up the EU (its 'Member States') remain independent sovereign nations but they pool their sovereignty in order to gain a strength and world influence none of them could have on their own. Pooling sovereignty means, in practice, that the Member States delegate some of their decision- making powers to shared institutions they have created, so that decisions on specific matters of joint interest can be made democratically at the European level. While the nation's pool their sovereignty, conflict and disunity arises as each nation responds protecting its own culture, people and industries"

The EU is a kingdom divided. While linked by the Treaty of Rome, each government still holds autonomy. The Member States speak their own languages and retain identity with their individual histories and cultures. EU citizens elect the leaders of the EU Parliament and Council of Ministers, and clay (i.e., the seed of men) represents this democratic practice. The EU's motto is "united in diversity," which literally can be the plaque underneath the image of toes mingled with clay. Due to the Union's many languages, which numbers 23 official languages, EU officials must make sure that all 27 Member States understand the legislation. They provide interpretation at many hundreds of meetings held every week. Twenty-five percent of university graduates employed by the Commission directly engage in language work. In the smaller Community institutions, this figure can be as high as 70 percent of graduates. Along with each new member accepted into the European Union, this number increases. The EU Parliament is the biggest employer of interpreters in the world employing 350 full time and 400 freelancers when there is higher demand.

Further magnifying the Union's diversity are each nation's differing governments and politics. Although the Union refers to the nations as Member States, they are separate sovereign countries. Some of the nations hold grievances with other nations, for historical or economic reasons. This world power will never have any real unity while it is both united and divided. In examining EU citizens' views and gripes toward other Member States, this division further intensifies. Nevertheless, Scripture tells us that this world power will be dreadful and terrible and exceedingly strong (Dan. 7:7).

These facts have caused some to believe that the EU will never have any real unity or strength. What the European Union is seeking to do has never been done in the world's history. Separate sovereign nations are joining to become a single economic and political unit. The Bible spoke about this in ancient history. In our day we will see it happen. We know from Scripture that the European Union federalists will attain economic and political union. The ideal of retaining each member state's government, language, and culture within this federation will be the weakness amid its strength.

13

THE EU TECHNOLOGY AGENDA

RACE networkRFlD is a European Union project which has been established to position the EU as a world leader in RFID excellence. The EU recognizes that RFID will increasingly influence the way people work and live and will bring great business opportunities and social benefits. It is therefore essential that Europe plays a leading role in shaping future developments. The vision of RACE networkRFlD is to provide a network of excellence that creates opportunities and increases the competitiveness of European Member States in the area of RFID thought leadership development and implementation.

THE EUROPEAN UNION AND THE MARK OF THE BEAST

"I want to talk about a very different revolution that is taking place right now, quietly sweeping the globe without bloodshed or conflict...Its effects are peaceful, but they will fundamentally alter our world, shatter old assumptions and reshape our lives...as its emblem, one might take the tiny silicon chip-no bigger than a fingerprint" Ronald Reagan

God commanded Ezekiel to place a mark on the foreheads of the men he would spare from the judgment inflicted on the wicked living in Jerusalem (Ez. 9:4). Revelation's 144,000 witnesses-12,000 men from each of the 12 tribes of Israel-each have God's seal on their foreheads (Rev. 9:4, 14:12). Paul, in his letters to the Corinthians and Ephesians, tells Christians that the Holy Spirit seals them. Therefore they will escape eternal hell fires (I Cor. 1:22, Eph. 1:13-14, 4:30). In the new heaven and earth, God dwells among man, and his servants have his name on their foreheads. Revelation 3:12 tells us:

"He who overcomes I will make him a pillar in the Temple of My God, and he shall go out no more; and I will write on him the name of My God, and the name of the city of My God, the New Jerusalem, which

comes down out of heaven from My God; and I will write on him My new name." Satan has always attempted to counterfeit God. His mark has been a characteristic of Satanism throughout the ages. According to Montague Summers, in her book The History of Witchcraft and Demonology:

" In 1661 the pupils of a cult confessed the Devil gives them a mark, which marks they renew as often as those persons have any desire to quit him. The Devil reproves them and more severely, and obligeth them to new promises, making them also new marks for assurance or pledge, that those persons should continue faithful to him. The Devil's mark to which allusion is here made, or the Witches' mark, as it is sometimes called, was regarded as perhaps the most important point in the identification of a witch, it was the very sign and seal of Satan upon the actual flesh of his servant, and any person who bore such a mark was considered to have been convicted and proven beyond all manner of doubt of being in league with and devoted to the service of the fiend"

During the Tribulation, Satan attempts to establish his kingdom here on the earth. His mark, on each of his followers, bears his name. According to Rev. 13:16-18:

"And he causes all, both small and great, rich and poor, free and slave, to receive a mark on their right hand, or on their forehead: And that no one may buy or sell, except one who has the mark, or the name of the beast, or the number of his name Here is wisdom. Let him who has understanding calculate the number of the beast: for it is the number of a man; and his number is 666"

The Antichrist will implement a system by which no man can buy or sell unless he wears a mark placed on his forehead or wrist. This etching in one's flesh represents the Beast or 666. Revelation refers to the mark in a spiritual context. Whosoever receives it spends eternity in hell (Rev. 14:11, 15:2, 19:20, 20:4). God punishes this abomination by sending a plague of foul and loathsome sores upon those who have the mark and worship the image (Rev. 16:2). Bible scholars theorize that the mark is part of a high-tech system that eliminates cash for the buying of goods. Thus, many evangelical theologians and students of prophecy follow the latest related technological developments, and note their possible evolution towards a cashless society. While this scenario provides one possible raison d'etre for the mark, other applications must not be excluded, such as high-tech identification and human tracking systems. The Antichrist launches this as both a technological breakthrough and a prerequisite for life in his totalitarian regime.

THE TECHNOLOGICAL RACE AMONG NATIONS

After careful examination of the prophetic writings, and considering the current global population, we can see that the Antichrist will not accomplish the Scriptural forecasts without technological breakthroughs. At no other time in history have science and technology made greater strides, or become a greater priority for nations than today.

The technological race replaced the Cold War as the new bandwagon of the superpowers. Today, technology is the key to national power. As Edward N. Luttwak, an American military strategist and historian theorized, we have gone "from geopolitics to geo-economics." He points out that methods of commerce have displaced military methods. Mr. Luttwak stated: "In this new era competitive technology projects are one of the weapons of commerce." The stake is what former Chancellor Helmut Schmidt once called the struggle for the world product, rather than for traditional power. The question occupying the nations of today is: who will win the technological race?

Studies over the past forty years have indicated that technological change is one of the most important factors that influence to a nation's rate of growth. A country's possession of knowledge has replaced its possession of natural resources as the key to economic prosperity. According to an EU Commission report on Science and Technology:

In this era of rapid technological change, the economic health of a region will depend on its capabilities to capture knowledge in science, technology and to foster innovation and entrepreneurship. Knowledge and its utilization are replacing the possession of a natural resource base as the key to economic prosperity and leadership. Any region which chooses to remain competitive in this next phase of the industrial revolution must adapt to this new order and devise mechanisms to exploit the economic potential of developed knowledge and technology.

For this reason, Japan aims to stay at least five years ahead of other countries in the development of new technologies. Nations now pursue the economic growth that new technologies can spur. From computers to television, consumers want the latest features. This fact has increased growth and spending in commercial research and development programs by Europe, the US, and Japan. This means that nations are in a race to promote new technological breakthroughs, and they work hard at making and selling the latest technologies. The European Union jumped on this bandwagon.

In 1974, the Council of Ministers decided to extend European Union research to the whole of science and technology, and instructed the Commission to implement several major research programs. In 1987, the European Union entered into the Single Act an article that gives the Union formal powers in the field of research and technology. It stated:

"The Communities' aim shall be to strengthen the scientific and technological basis of European industry and to encourage it to become more competitive at the international level....it shall encourage undertakings to exploit the Community's internal market to the full."

Today, scientific research is the third largest area of EU spending, after agriculture and structural development. Information technology heads the list of basic areas of future research programs. The Federal Trust for Education and Research, a think-tank organization that aids in formulating EU policy, stated in a report that:

"Europe cannot afford to exclude itself from the profound technological transformation which is currently sweeping the world and which is expected to be the locomotive of economic development over the next two or three decades. Historians have noted that, periodically, the world brings forth a new technology, or group of related technologies, of such a revolutionary nature that it transforms the whole basis of economic activity...There is little disagreement that information technology is the mainstream technology of the current era"

One cannot help but wonder if the EU will herald the Mark of the Beast as a technology of "a revolutionary nature, "to transform the world economy.

THE COMMISSION'S RTD NETWORK

Although the Mark of the Beast exists, the Antichrist must be in a political position that provides him direct access to technological programs and the power to implement them. We have established that the Commission presidency holds the seat of the Antichrist. The Commission presently oversees all research and technological development (RTD) programs in the European Union. It proposes, initiates, and implements RTD decisions. This gives the Commission direct and total control over technological projects. The Commission can even propose and suggest their own ideas. This will be the case with the Beast's mark.

The Commission has its own network. Various groups of specialized Commission officials manage the Union's RTD programs. These men, scientists by training, often come from university laboratories or industrial research centers. From their central position, they do much to speed up the circulation of ideas and the dissemination of knowledge.

Three of the most important committees with general responsibilities include CREST, CODEST, and IRDAK. CREST, the Committee for Scientific and Technical Research, consists of senior officials liable for scientific policy. It advises both the Commission and the Council of the European Union. CODEST, the Committee for the European Development for Science and Technology, enlists twenty-four members who are leaders from the scientific world. IRDAC, the Industrial Research and Development Advisory Committee, includes representatives from European industry. The advisory committees for each of the sectors concerned aid in the preparation and use of the individual programs.

One of the Commission's Vice President's is in charge of RTD. Other commissioners have the task of overseeing the individual research programs. One overlooks the development and use of advanced technology and the activities of IRDAC, while others are in scientific and technical cooperation with European Free Trade Association (EFTA) and non-member countries. This internal network will give the Antichrist direct access to new technologies. The key RTD program devised by the Commission to create a technological base to compete with the US and Japan is ESPRIT: The European Strategic Program for Research and Development in Information Technology. The Commission launched it in 1984. The Commission must approve the selected projects. Proposed projects that have strategic and commercial importance receive money. Concerning the ESPRIT program, the Commission wrote in the mid 1980's:

"In world trade, electronic equipment will overtake the automobile sector in the 1990's with worldwide R&D spending on information technologies rising from $35 billion in 1986 to some $90 billion in 1990. It will remain one of the dominant sources of technological advance until the end of the century ...information, in all its forms to become both one of the leading international commodities in itself and a vital element of economic activity in general. And it is rapidly becoming a driving force for social change....Information technology is therefore of key importance to the economy, both in renewing the competitiveness of established sectors and in the new opportunities it offers for a Europe rich in information skills. For Europe to make the most of opportunities offered by information technology requires strategic action....The blueprint for this emerging European Technology Community has been established in the 1980's with the European Strategic Program for Research and Development in Information Technology"

One of ESPRIT's projects deals with payment cards and electronic purses. Commission officials are testing the cards. In the same way the future officials will test the Mark of the Beast. The European Union also has links with many countries through bilateral agreements on scientific and technical cooperation. These include major industrial powers such as the US, Japan, and Canada. They also admit the new industrialized Third World countries (Mexico, Brazil, India). The EU also maintains permanent relations with other international organizations active in research, such as the specialized UN agencies. As President of the Commission, the Antichrist will have knowledge of recent developments, and will support programs that suit his policies.

The Commission decides who will buy and sell with the Union. The Union will incorporate the "Mark of the Beast," i.e., this technological system, into EU financial policy. The mark will serve several purposes. Despite the economic benefits and other rhetoric, the technology will mainly act to mark his citizens and monitor them in his dictatorship.

REPLACING THE CASH SYSTEM

The mark will not just happen one day; it will not occur overnight. The system's rise will occur as a gradual order of events. Prior to buying and selling with the mark, financial experts will campaign for a cashless society. This is already happening. An international consortium of market leaders which aims for a "no cash" economy has formed in the payments industry, to develop standards for a new way to pay by "electronic purse." Consumers use this card with a microcomputer instead of cash or checks when paying. The aim is to use it for everything from vending machines and public transportation to traditional passports and pay telephones. A pan-European consortium of consultants, academic institutions, and technology companies put together the EU-backed system. Banks can use the "smart cards" for many uses such as an alternative to traditional passports and credit cards, and as a method of payment for payphones, taxis, shops, and vending machines. Even police spot-checks in the EU will use an integrated system of identification using machine-readable ID cards. Smart cards and electronic purses will lay the groundwork for the Beast's mark.

Payment cards and electronic banking will replace the cash system. Prompting this change is the enormous cost of paperwork. Prior to the wide use of the internet, the US spent $30 billion per year to process nearly 40 billion checks. In international trade, paperwork costs range between 4 and 15 percent of the value of the merchandise. Electronic data interchange reduces these costs. The Internet has added its contribution to reducing these costs and also by offering online shopping, banking and payments debited directly out of one's bank account to pay credit cards, utilities, taxes and mortgages.

The EU plans to develop a "European Nervous System" that would connect government computers in the EU nations, to transfer data about everything from taxes to pollution levels. This nervous system will no doubt be in place before the mark is developed. The system has the potential to connect worldwide. The Antichrist will use such a system to keep track of all the marked individuals. There is also another Biblical parallel here. God's Holy Spirit indwells each Christian, and connects them (so to speak) to Jesus through his Spirit. Computers will act as the counterfeit to the Holy Spirit. As the Christian connects to the body of Jesus, the individual living during the Tribulation will connect to the Beast's "central nervous system," i.e., computers.

The devices that will become the Mark of the Beast already exist. Companies call them bio-implants. Bio-implants are now available for the identification of animals and the medical field uses them in humans for patient identification. A veterinarian places it beneath the animal's skin, and it contains information about the pet and his owner. The company VeriChip sold them to a Barcelona nightclub which used them for 125 patrons who used their chip as a debit card to debit drinks.

Verichip received FDA approval in 2004 as implantable radio-frequency identification (RFID) microchip. Twice the length of a dime the medical technician implants it between the shoulder and elbow of an individual's right arm. Once scanned it responds with a unique 16 digit number which links to information about the user held on a database for identity verification, medical records access and other uses. A doctor or medical practitioner performs the insertion procedure under local anesthetic in a physician's office. In the beginning of 2007, Verichip Corporation created Xmark, its corporate identity for healthcare products. Xmark incorporates Hugs and the Halo system of infant protection: the RoamAlert system of wandering protection; the MyCall emergency response system; and the Assetrac asset tracking system.

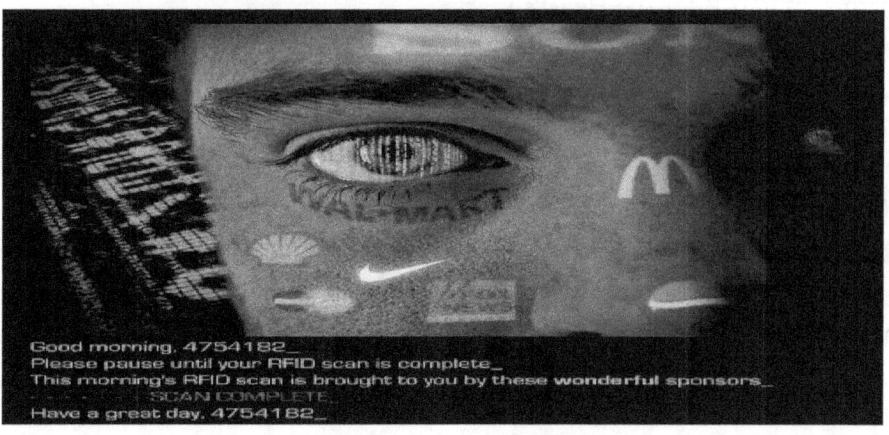

An implant in the wrist or forehead of a human individual will become the future use of this technology. It will be able to carry all kinds of data about an individual. With child abductions a concern, and with heightened security since September 11, 2001, and the advent of the war on terror; implants will offer a great appeal. The new technology will also create jobs and contribute to economic growth. The Antichrist will use the mark to monitor those in his police state and even more so by taking the mark the individual will pledge their allegiance to his authority and ideology.

THE MARRIAGE OF MAN TO COMPUTERS

EU Scientists call it "Adaptive Brain Interface (ABI), and the EU's ESPRIT program funds and sponsors its development. An individual hooked up to a computer can give the computer commands by his mind alone. Although the immediate application for ABI is to help the physically impaired, as this technology further develops, its potential within a police state is almost unimaginable. In March 2000, in Brussels, a paraplegic named Gabriele Taonconi demonstrated before EU officials his ability to walk thanks to a computer chip implanted near his spine and wired to his legs. They postponed his demonstration because of a computer glitch that prevented commands from communicating to the computer chip. Professor Pierre Rabi Schong of Montpellier University of France, a project coordinator, said the implanted chip allows the user to create artificial muscle movement.

"We are trying to reproduce what happens in the brain…with electrodes to nerves and muscles."

MEDIA INSIGHT (WWW.UCL.CO.UK)
HUMAN BRAIN PROJECT WINS MAJOR EU FUNDING

The Human Brain Project has been officially selected as one of the European Commission's two FET Flagship projects. The new project will unite European efforts to address one of the greatest challenges of modern science: understanding the human brain.

The goal of the Human Brain Project is to pull together all our existing knowledge about the human brain and to reconstruct the brain, piece by piece, in supercomputer-based models and simulations. The models offer the prospect of a new understanding of the human brain and its diseases and of completely new computing and robotic technologies.

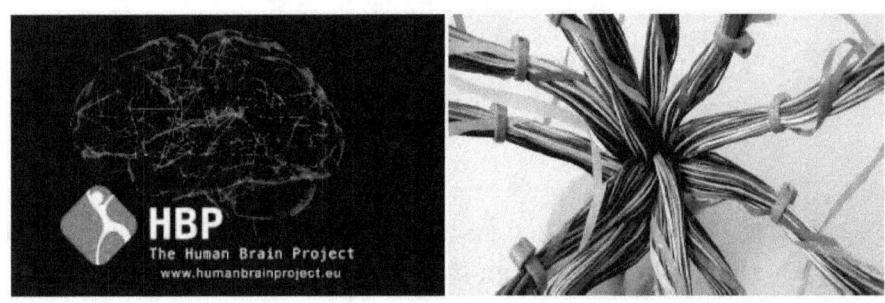

The Human Brain Project is planned to last ten years (2013-2023). The cost is estimated at 1.19 billion euros.

More than 80 European and international research institutions are involved in the project, including UCL groups led by Professor Alex Thomson (UCL School of Pharmacy), Professor Neil Burgess (UCL Institute of Cognitive Neuroscience) and Professor John Ashburner (UCL Institute of Neurology).

The project will also associate some important North American and Japanese partners. It will be coordinated at the Ecole Polytechnique Federale de Lausanne (EPFL) in Switzerland, by neuroscientist Henry Markram with co-directors Karlheinz Meier of Heidelberg University, Germany, and Richard Frackowiak (a former UCL Vice-Provost) from the Centre Hospitalier Universitaire Vaudois (CHUV) and the University of Lausanne (UNIL).

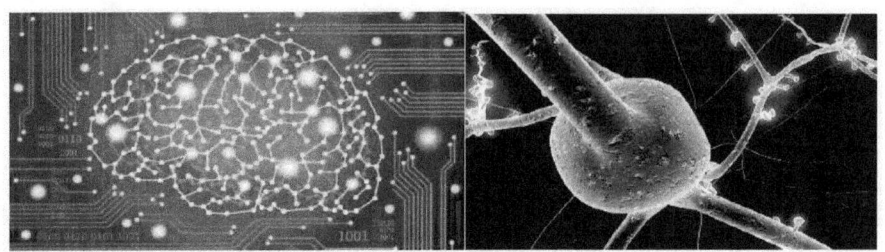

MEDIA INSIGHT (WWW.UCL.CO.UK)

HUMAN BRAIN PROJECT WINS MAJOR EU FUNDING

Professor Malcolm Grant, UCL President & Provost, said: "By funding the Human Brain Project the European Commission has proved their commitment to funding large scale science research. UCL's role in the Human Brain Project will strengthen and further develop the world-leading research already underway here in the fields of neurology and neuroscience."

Researchers hope to better understand the energy efficiency of the human brain, and use this knowledge towards the development of biologically inspired computers. Such devices could have a major impact on industry.

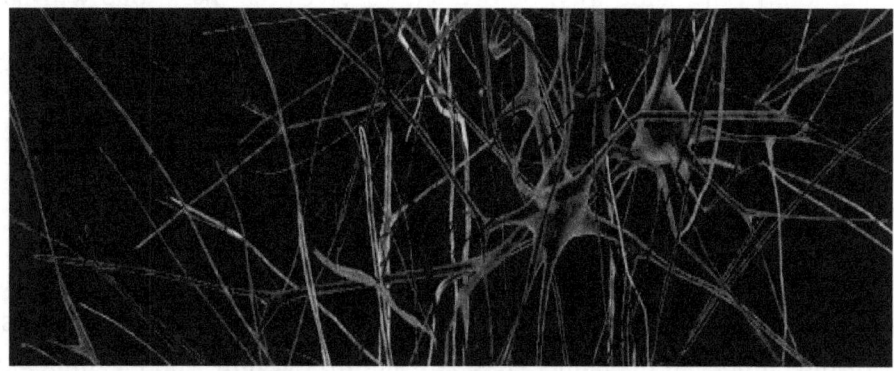

Another major goal of the Human Brain Project is to generate tools and infrastructure for the research community and catalyze the development of new treatments for brain disease.

The Human Brain Project is the world's largest brain research program and more than 20 UK research teams in academia and industry will be involved in the start of the project.

The selection of the Human Brain Project as a FET Flagship is the result of more than three years of preparation and a rigorous and severe evaluation by a large panel of independent, high profile scientists, chosen by the European Commission.

Eventually a computer chip will not only track one's movements, but control individuals, reducing men to robots performing acts against their will. Never before in history have new technologies moved to the forefront of national policies. The European Union is able to research, develop, and, through the Commission, implement whatever system it chooses. The Antichrist will enter his position in a world market where the development of new technologies governs economic growth. Initially, the system will offer all kinds of economic and social benefits. With a secured identification system for buying and selling, all kinds of crimes will diminish. Those who receive the mark will suffer the wrath of God. The Bible predicts the horrific side effect of grievous sores that breaks out on the bodies of the implanted. The Antichrist will not just implement the system for economic and social benefits; this is his mark, his label on those he rules. It will act as his tie to them, and it counterfeits God's seal of redemption. The born-again Christian must accept the good news of the Gospel before he receives the Holy Spirit and God's seal of redemption. In the same way, before one receives the mark, one will have to accept the Antichrist's gospel concerning his deity.

THE NUMBER OF HIS NAME

The Book of Revelation provides the one riddle found in Scripture and it concerns the identity of the Beast. Revelation 13:17-18 states: "and that no one may buy or sell except one who has the mark or the name of the beast or the number of his name. Here is wisdom. Let him who has understanding calculate the number of the beast, for it is the number of a man: His number is 666."

The Mark is also the name of the Beast who is a man. Scripture names no other man with a number except Antichrist who God assigns the number 666. The two other times the number 666 is used in Scripture is mentioned in 1 Kings 10:14 and 2 Chr. 9:13. The Bible tells us that after the Queen of Sheba's visit, Solomon yearly took in 666 talents of gold from the surrounding nations. Deuteronomy 17:15-17 warns that a king of Israel shall not multiply wives, silver or gold which Solomon did in addition to going after the gods of his foreign wives and building high places for them. 1 Kings Chapter 11 describes Solomon's descent into idolatry.

In addition, Nebuchadnezzar's idolatrous golden image was 60 cubits high by 6 cubits wide, thus 66. Throughout history, ancient and modern nations use gold for currency. Only after World War II did the world stop using gold as a reserve for currencies. Gold, i.e. money is synonymous with idolatry. The number calculates to his name and relates to the currency system under the Antichrist, which he ties into his dictatorship and his blasphemous identity. He will cause the world to worship him and commit mass idolatry. The riddle which will be solved during the Tribulation further identifies him as the son of Satan and his mark as the means by which one gives one's soul to the Devil and ends any hope of redemption.

The start of the Tribulation ends the age of grace and ushers in a final dispensation. The Beast's government while rich and powerful becomes a monotheistic dictatorship with the worship and adoration to the State and its leader. The wheat and the tares divide into two categories of persons; those who take the Mark of the Beast and those who say no. Those who do not take the Mark of the Beast will refuse because of their belief in the true God and His Son Jesus Christ.

CHANGING OF THE GUARD

One of the consequences of the financial upheaval of 2008 and 2009, reported the U.S. newsmagazine BusinessWeek, is that Europe is now richer than North America. The accumulated national wealth of North Americans has dropped by 21.8 percent while Europe's only fell by 5.8 percent, "down to 22.2 trillion euros-a quarter of the globe's total wealth" ("Europe Now Richer Than North America," BusinessWeek, Sept. 16, 2009). As great wealth is necessary for global power, could Europe be on the verge of taking over from the United States? Bible prophecy shows that a new, European-centered superpower will exist immediately before Jesus Christ's return. It will be a great commercial system whose trade dominates the world. It will change the future global economic order.

14

THE US-EU PARTNERSHIP

Of the "latter day" nations mentioned in the Scriptures, America receives no direct citation, except possibly in two passages. For those who live during America's present era of prosperity and strength, this fact is puzzling. Some experts solve this puzzle by teaching that America is Babylon, and Jeremiah foretells its destruction. Babylon represents the European Union. Given that the Union becomes the most powerful world empire to ever exist, the United States must lose its sole superpower status in the interim. Since the entire world worships the Beast, it is safe to conclude that the US will remain in a strong alliance with the EU.

America is the daughter country of its mother Europe. Without America, the EU would never have united. The unified Europe of 1992 evolved, perhaps inevitably, from the Marshall Plan. American leaders of the postwar period believed that a strong, independent Europe stood in the best long-term interest of the United States. The US supplied Europe with the funds to rebuild itself, and even provided for its defense against Communist forces in postwar Europe.

Since the 1950s, the United States has consistently supported the Union's development. A stronger and more united Europe can share the burden of global responsibilities. Conservative President Ronald

Reagan stated to the European Parliament in 1985: "We continue to see a strong and unified Europe not as a rival, but as an ever stronger partner."

The Bush Sr. Administration gave greater priority to improving ties with the Union than any previous American administration. Former President Bush Sr. stated that "a stronger Europe, a more united Europe, is good for my country, and it is a development to be welcomed, a natural evolution with an alliance, the product of true partnership, 40 years in the making." Bush viewed Europe as "a partner in world leadership." He stated that he believed that a strong, united Europe meant a strong America. George Bush's administration upgraded the diplomatic status of the EU Commission in Washington. President Bush strongly supported the Common Market. He urged the EU to continue with intense efforts towards European Unity.

After the fall of the Berlin Wall, the European Union became the "cornerstone" for the new European architecture. These changes strengthened the EU's desire to speed unification and assume its newfound role as a political leader. The US encouraged such a role as a major step toward the kind of global "burden sharing" it has long urged upon its European allies. Former US Secretary of State James Baker proposed "that the United States and the European Union work together to achieve, whether in treaty or some other form, a significantly strengthened set of institutional and consultative links." Baker believed that since the US and EU shared common ideals and values, and both faced the same challenges in economics, foreign policy, and a host of other fields, it was a matter of common course for both governments to work together.

The EU is America's most important trading partner. Their combined GDP is around 60% of the world total while they constitute only around 10% of the world's population. Together they account for 40% all world trade. They form the largest trading partnership in the world. The political, economic, and corporate links between the two are broad and deep. Even more important is their cumulative mutual investment stake in each other's economy.

Europe's investment in the US represents 75% of all European investment abroad and roughly 60% for all foreign direct investment in the United States. By 2001, the US investment stake in Europe grew to roughly half of all US investment abroad, and in 2001, this investment yielded half of all foreign earnings for US companies. Each has a significant stake in the prosperity of the other. For this reason former EU Commission President Jacques Delors called for a new and profound partnership between the EU and the United States.

An EU Economic Affairs Commissioner in the 1990's made it clear that a stronger and larger EU would be in the best interest of the US. According to the Commissioner, by the end of the 1990s, Europe would be a political and economic entity with a crucial role, as a major engine of the world economy and as a stabilizing factor in world affairs. He believed that it was in America's best interest that this evolution continues with as little friction as possible. He assumed the US would lend this process its full moral and political force. The EU's new role will present the US with a challenge. Experts believe that the American ability to influence the policies of the European Union will decline.

Former President Clinton noted that he felt more favorably than his predecessors about "European Unity and…the European defense capacity to greater strength and unity within Europe." He labeled Germany as the leader of Europe, and as the privileged partner of the US. Clinton viewed the Union as "America's most valued partner in trade and investment." He believed that a "strong and more unified Europe makes for a more effective economic and political partner."

THE TRANS-ATLANTIC DECLARATION

In 1990, the US and EU agreed to strengthen their relations, when both sides signed the "Trans-Atlantic Declaration." The US President and the Presidents of the European Council and EU Commission agreed to meet twice a year, and the US-EU relationship continues to evolve. At each summit, the EU and US set further goals for cooperation and joint action.

In 1995, the US and EU agreed to work together in promoting peace and democracy worldwide. Issues on their agenda are international crime, drug trafficking, terrorism, refuge problems, environmental damage, and the spread of infectious diseases. They also pledged to support the Middle East peace process, and to commit to developing a full and equal partnership. Initially, leaders met to create the world's largest free trade zone. Instead, defense and social issues came to the forefront.

In 1997, the EU and US intensified their cooperation on key foreign policy issues, and made progress in issues of world trade and other global concerns. They signed the "Science and Technology and Cooperation Agreement," which promotes closer cooperation between EU and US scientists and scientific institutions.

In 1998, the EU and US turned their attention to the new trans-Atlantic marketplace, after recognizing that they shared the world's largest and most complex economic relationship (each accounting for half of the other's foreign investment abroad), and that the prosperity of their populations intertwined. They decided that it was their task to work together to maintain open markets, and sustain the momentum of liberalization. They agreed to pursue their objectives together through the World Trade Organization, and renewed their commitment to political and economic support of the Middle East peace process. The EU and the US launched the Transatlantic Economic Partnership (TEP) at the London summit in May 1998.

In 1999, the EU and US added small arms and light weapons control to their agenda, and agreed that the destabilizing accumulation and spread of such weapons demanded the urgent attention of the international community. In the Bonn Declaration adopted at the 1999 EU-US summit in Bonn, both sides committed themselves to a "full and equal partnership" in economic, political and security affairs. The next year, the EU and US agreed to work on accelerated action to combat AIDS in Africa, and continued to discuss the development of their joint role as peacekeepers. They committed to the construction of a new European Security Architecture in which NATO, the EU, the Western European Union (WEU), the Organization for Security and Cooperation in Europe (OSCE), and the Council of Europe would have complementary and mutually reinforcing roles to play.

At their 2001 summit, the EU and US discussed how they might use their partnership to solve trade disputes, and to promote peace and stability throughout the world. The US welcomed the efforts of the EU to acquire a civilian and military crisis management capability, which would reinforce the Union's ability to contribute to international peace. They also agreed to strengthen and revitalize the UN. In May of 2002, the EU and US held a Quartet meeting that also included the UN and Russian Federation, to work jointly in support of a secure and lasting peace in the Middle East.

At the 2007 EU-US summit, leaders formed the Transatlantic Economic Integration Framework, creating the Transatlantic Economic Council (TEC). In the economic area the EU and the US mostly work together within the framework of the Transatlantic Economic Partnership and under the multilateral umbrella of the WTO. They conducted a number of dialogues. The transatlantic business dialogue, a transatlantic labor dialogue, a consumer dialogue, an environmental dialogue and also the European Parliament/US Congress and Senate legislative dialogue. Other important projects such as the EU Centers in the US are also included under this section

.

The European Union and the United States are the two largest economies in the world. They account together for about half the entire world economy. The EU and the US have also the biggest bilateral trading and investment relationship. Transatlantic flows of trade and investment amount to around $1 billion a day, and, jointly, their global trade accounts for almost 40% of world trade. With so much invested in each other's economies the ties between both continents so deep their partnership will only continue to deepen. The EU-US partnership does not imply that all leaders and political experts view the EU as an entity of light. Conservative spokespersons such as Pat Buchanan, and magazines of conservative thought and opinion such as National Review, speak out against a federal united Europe. Their views reflect Thatcher's position against bureaucratic centralism or a superstate that will rule all of

Europe.

THE DECLINE OF THE US

With the rise of the EU to world empire status one cannot help but ask of the US's position and standing alongside this final power. As the EU rises to superpower status, the role of the US will decline. Some say this decline has already begun. Jacques Attali, the former president of the Bank for Reconstruction and Development, referred to Bush's victory in the Gulf War as the "last hurrah of a weakening global power." The US's influence is declining and America is eroding from within. Drugs and crime, are rampant. Its families are falling apart, and its educational system produces test scores at an all-time low. According to a writer for the Academy of Political Science:

"It has become cliché to say that unsatisfactory economic performance is undermining the United States' global leadership position. The budget deficit, trade deficit, and the need to finance these deficits with a large inflow of foreign capital into the United States have seriously weakened the American claim to global economic leadership-and possibly to political leadership as well."

This deficit exploded with the onset of the Great Recession. The dollar is no longer the world's most stable currency. It has become a source of uncertainty and instability in the world economy. The US debt burden is so great that at the time of the fall of the Berlin Wall, aid to Eastern Europe on the scale of the Marshall Plan had become impossible. EU countries led by Germany made the main contributions. America's economic position will decline further as Asia and Europe continue to grow more rapidly than the US. Zbigniew Brzezinski commented in the last decade: "Unless America pays more attention to its domestic weaknesses, a new global pecking order could emerge early in the next century, in the event that a unifying Europe and an economically dynamic Japan were to assume large political and military responsibilities."

In the Gulf War, the US had to rely on the political and financial support of other countries. A New York Times editorial stated: "Superpowers can afford to pay for their own wars; we cannot."

Some experts argue that the United States needs a new vision of its role in the world, and that it will have less and less influence in world affairs. Walter Russell Mead, senior fellow for international economics of the World Policy Institute, cited events that prove America's decline and the erosion of its influence. He stated: "The East European countries decided to link their new trading regime to the European monetary system, rather than to the dollar. Sweden… took the dollar out of the basket of currencies against which the Kroner would float and based its value directly to EC currencies. Poland, too, downgraded the dollar. The formerly Communist countries…It was to Bonn first and to Brussels second that they would turn for assistance, guidance, and models of economic and political behavior.

...For the first time, prominent European financial and political leaders could be heard to say that Washington was a nonentity. ... Jacques Atali, head of the European Bank for Reconstruction and development, spoke dismissively of the United States as a failed nation; he argued that the great struggle of the future would be the battle between Europe and Japan for the global leadership that Washington had already and irretrievably lost"

The Europeans are creating a new Europe centered on the EU. They do not see the US as a partner in this process. In the early 1990's commentators such as Lionel Barber, the editor of the Financial Times who then served as the Washington correspondent for the newspaper, commented: "Plenty of signs indicate that the United States will find it difficult to adjust to the 'New World Order' in which Washington's leadership is open to challenge." It was speculated that "the US will be a major player in the world economy but not a dominant one, and that it will achieve its goals only as part of a consensus with other countries."

At the same time, Dominique Moisi, who was acting as the Associate Director of the Institute Francais Des Relations Internationales, predicted: "The American Century is coming to an end. The United States will undoubtedly remain the strongest power in the community of North Atlantic democracies, but its days as a hegemonic and sole protective power for Europe are counted." Mr. Moisi believed that "it is unlikely even that the twenty-first century will be dubbed, like the twentieth, the American Century.....The US has neither the desire nor the means to recapture that privileged moment it experienced after the Second World War. We are witnessing a transitional stage in the international system....The role of the US will remain crucial, but it will stand alongside the other powers, and will no longer be alone in its category."

The US's position further deteriorated the first decade of the millennium. Since the millennium, the United States has fought two wars and funded the disasters left behind from the devastating hurricanes which included hurricane Katrina, which nearly sunk New Orleans. In addition the US funded the bailout for the Great Recession. The US deficit is now in the trillions. In 2009 the US deficit reached 12.3 % of the nation's GDP. The Financial Crisis which started with the US subprime mortgage market caused a domino effect around the globe and the loss of confidence of global powers in the US Financial system. From the BBC to the Financial Times, leading news services quoted experts who said that the US's role as the leading superpower changed and would not be the same after the financial crisis. That the world was now multipolar with the emergence of better capitalized centers in Asia and Europe.

Former Belgian Prime Minister and EU Parliamentarian Guy Verhofstadt, summed up perfectly in his essay, "The Financial Crisis - Three Ways Out for Europe:"

"The economic downturn in the West, and particularly the United States, will undoubtedly also cast a shadow over the former's political dominance in the world. Not that this dominance will suddenly collapse: the power of the US, in particular, is too great and too multifaceted for that. Put another way, America's absolute power will remain huge into the near future, but its relative power will crumble, thereby shifting the balance of power. For whereas the weight of other nations and blocks (China, India, Russia, Brazil, etc.) is increasing that of the United States has quite clearly reached its peak"

The dollar's decline is causing alarm for many countries that peg their currencies to the dollar and for countries that hold sizeable positions of US assets. Financial experts are questioning the dollar's status as a global reserve currency. In addition no one knows the long term results of President Obama's bailout plan, or the possible consequences of the US printing more money to fund the bail out. Quantitative easing i.e. the printing of money, if not done properly can destroy an economy by causing inflation and devaluing its currency. The policy destroyed the nation of Zimbabwe.

The aftermath of the Great Recession will change the global pecking order and the US will lose its position as the leading nation in the world. The BBC reported in 2008, that "the US Superpower Status is Shaken." They quoted political philosopher John Gray and former professor at the London School of Economics as writing in the London paper, The Observer:

"Here is a historic geopolitical shift, in which the balance of power in the world is being altered irrevocably…The era of American global leadership, reaching back to the Second World War, is over…The American free-market creed has self- destructed while countries that retained overall control of markets have been vindicated…In a change as far-reaching in its implications as the fall of the Soviet Union, an entire model of government and the economy has collapsed…How symbolic that Chinese astronauts take a spacewalk while the US Treasury Secretary is on his knees"

Even the Financial Times, the world's leading financial newspaper reported that "the US will lose its role as a global financial "superpower" in the wake of the financial crisis. The article quoted German finance minister Peer Steinbruck as blaming Washington for failing to take the regulatory steps that might have prevented the crisis. He stated:

"The US will lose its status as the superpower of the world financial system. This world will become multipolar with the emergence of stronger, better capitalized centers in Asia and Europe, the world will never be the same again…if we look back 10 years from now, we will see 2008 as a fundamental rupture."

Director of National Intelligence, Dennis Blair, told Congress that instability in countries around the world caused by the global economic crisis and its geopolitical implications, rather than terrorism, is the primary near-term security threat to the United States. Paul Craig Roberts who was Assistant Secretary of the Treasury in the Reagan administration and Assistant Editor of the Wall Street Journal summarized the US economy in his article, "The Dollar's Reserve Currency Role is Drawing to an End," and commented that the US's economic profile is that of a third world economy. According to Mr. Roberts:"If the US government cannot balance its budget by cutting its spending or by raising taxes, the day when it can no longer borrow will see the government paying its bills by printing money like a third world banana republic. Inflation and more exchange rate depreciation will be the order of the day."

If all of this is not bleak enough, Fred Bergstein, the Director of the economic think-tank The Peterson Institute, wrote in Foreign Affairs: "The Peterson Institute for International Economics projects that the international economic position of the United States is likely to deteriorate enormously as a result, with the current account deficit rising from a previous record of six percent of GDP to over 15 percent (more than $5 trillion annually) by 2030 and net debt climbing from $3.5 trillion today to $50 trillion (the equivalent of 140 percent of GDP and more than 700 percent of exports) by 2030. The United States would then be transferring a full seven percent ($2.5 trillion) of its entire economic output to foreigners every year in order to service its external debt"

THE RISE OF THE ALMIGHTY EURO AND THE FALL OF THE DOLLAR

The Great Recession prompted by the financial crisis and America's enormous deficit is affecting America's greatest asset: the US Dollar. The US dollar has been the most widely held currency in the world and it stood as symbol of US strength and prosperity. It is the world's reserve or anchor currency, this means that many governments and institutions used the dollar as part of their foreign exchange reserves. This number totaled about two thirds of the allocated reserves. The dollar became the international pricing currency for products traded on the global market such as oil and gold. This allowed the US to purchase the commodities at a marginally lower rate than other nations and to borrow at a better rate because there existed such a large market for the dollar. This allowed the US to run its high trade deficits and greatly postponed the economic impact. The dollar has been losing its role as the reserve currency and as Mr. Roberts noted above, "The Dollar's Reserve Currency Role is Drawing to an End." The dollar's loss of its reserve status will have terrible effects on the US economy. If the dollar looses it status of reserve currency, the US as we know it will be no more. According to financial guru Michael Murphy:

"The US government will have less economic leeway to deal with the current financial mess, because excess Federal debt creation will lead immediately to a lower dollar and higher imported inflation. Longer term, the government will have to find another way to pay its debts than just selling Treasuries to the Fed. Most likely, they will have no choice. The price of gold and silver will go up as they are used more as a currency asset, competitive with the world and regional currencies. The price of oil and all other internationally traded commodities will go up in most currencies, and go up a lot in US dollars. American lifestyles and financial habits will be forced to change radically in a world where we have to pay as we go. Longer term, economic power and wealth will shift from the West to the East and, to a lesser extent, the Middle East. The US government will have no choice but to tax US citizens and businesses more heavily"

While the US dollar erodes, the euro since its launch in 1999 has risen to become the second largest currency holding of foreign reserves. As early as 2007 Alan Greenspan was quoted in a weekly German magazine Stern saying it was "absolutely conceivable that the euro will replace the dollar as the dominate foreign reserve currency, or will be traded as an equally important reserve currency."

According to Vanessa Cross a business writer, who wrote "Can the Euro Replace Dollar as Dominate Foreign Reserve Currency," in supporting her view she quoted econometric analysis by Jeffrey Frankel and Menzie Chinn who indicated that the euro could replace the US dollar as the major reserve currency by 2020 if the dollar continued to depreciate and if the UK adopted the euro by 2020. She also noted the so-called BRIC nations - Brazil, Russia, India, and China - demanding the establishment of an international currency and for the dollar's replacement as the world's benchmark currency. China suggested that a new currency reserve system controlled by the International Monetary Fund (IMF) would be more stable.

In September of 2009, the UN followed China and Russia and called for a new global currency to replace the dollar. The US dollar is not Russia's basic reserve currency anymore. The euro-based share of reserve assets of Russia's Central Bank increased to the level of 47.5 percent as of January 1, 2009 and exceeded the investments in dollar assets, which made up 41.5 percent. Also in September of 2009, The New York Times reported that Robert Zoelick president of the World Bank came out and said that America's days as an unchallenged economic superpower might be numbered and that the dollar was likely to lose its favored position as the euro and the Chinese renminbi assumed bigger roles.

He added that the euro provided a "respectable alternative" for financing international transactions and that there was "every reason to believe that the euro's acceptability could grow." According to former Federal Reserve Chairman Alan Greenspan the dollar no longer had much of a lead over the euro, he said, adding that the European Central Bank had "developed into a global economic force to be taken seriously."

Ambassador Günter Burghardt, Head of the Delegation of the European Commission to the United States, noted in a speech to the Federal Reserve Bank in Atlanta Georgia, in as early as 2003, that "the euro has established itself as the second-most important currency after the US dollar on the world's financial markets."

He noted that in 2003 the outstanding amount of bonds and notes in euros increased to 41% compared to the US's 43%, and the euro's money market instruments rose to almost 46%. Also by 2003 over 50 countries operated and managed exchange-rate arrangements that include the euro as a reference. Meanwhile banks around the world such as the Central Bank of Russia, the Bank of Canada, central banks in Asia, Taiwan, Singapore and China have increased their euro holdings. He added that "the European Central Bank itself contributes to the prevailing role of the US currency as the official reserve currency."

Mr. Burghardt also pointed out in that speech that: "This enhanced profile in the monetary sphere has not yet translated into an appropriate external representation of the euro area. Despite the fact that the euro area today is the largest trading partner, main aid donor and second largest GDP producer in the world, its influence in the shaping of global economic decisions does not yet correspond to those capabilities. To borrow and American analogy, we are punching far below our weight"

We know from Scripture and in reviewing the climate within the EU that the day is coming when the EU will assert itself on the world stage. The Secretary General of the Union of European Federalists, Joan- Marc Simon reiterated and summarized what European think-tanks and leaders have been stating when she wrote: "The 20th century has seen the rise and consolidation of the US as the world superpower which has been interlinked with the establishment of the dollar as the world currency. The current economic crisis, with the US decline and the emergence of new world powers, is leading towards a multipolar world and this will result in a new world monetary order which will re-shape economics, internal policies and international relations for years to come. During the last decades the US has been exploiting the condition of the dollar as a reserve currency to run colossal deficits in its trade and current-accounts with which it has financed its economy and has managed to keep its status of the world superpower. This time it looks like the dollar domination is over and during next years most probably we will assist to the birth of a new monetary world order"

There are other variables that will also come into play such as the European Central Bank greatly reducing its dollar holdings, and other nations that will join the euro increasing its strength. When the dollar ceases to be the world reserve currency, this will officially mark the end of the US as the leading superpower. The economic impact will once again affect the global marketplace.

Spain's former Secretary of State of Economy and Secretary General of Commerce, Guillermo de la Dehesa wrote an article questioning if the euro will ever replace the dollar as the reserve currency. He pointed out that if the UK joined the euro, given London's position as one of the world's two leading financial markets both in Euros and US Dollars, and because it has the EU's second largest GDP after Germany, this would provide a major boost to the euro. He stated that the EU's present union is a handicap because the EU is not an actual federal state but a union of independent nations. We know from Scripture this will change especially when the Union moves forward with its political core of members.

MEDIA INSIGHT (WASHINGTON POST)
ANNE APPLEBAUM ON EUROPE: THE WORLD'S NEW SUPERPOWER

Fortunately, there is another power that shares America's economic and political values, that possesses sophisticated military technology and is also very interested in stopping the progress of fanatical movements, especially in North Africa and the Middle East. That power is Europe.

THE NEXT SUPERPOWER

Ironically, in the early 1990's, the US became concerned that Japan would become a dominant power that would undermine the economic security of the US and Europe by the middle of the next century. A CIA report stated: "Japan is a fundamentally amoral society that will dominate the world through its economic power." At the time, The Economist stated that "while Americans fret over whether Japan will overtake them as an economic power, Uncle Sam is more likely to be knocked off his pedestal by the European Community." The article pointed out that the EU's population is a third larger than America's, and that the EU, taken as a whole, is the world's biggest exporter. Where America will take its biggest knock is at the IMF and the World Bank. Under institutional rules, the headquarters of these institutions are located in the territory of the member nation with the biggest quota. The headquarters will one day move from Washington to Brussels and The EU will have the dominant role in world economic management under the Antichrist.

European leaders have spoken out against Pax Americana, the American determination to enforce a worldwide peace. They observe that the UN and Europe could counterbalance what they view as the imperial outreach of the US. Europe will go beyond counterbalancing the US; it will be aiding the US's economy through its policies. America views the Common Market as a bolster to the US economy. America, who once shouldered the world's problems, views a burden-sharing Europe as a benefit. The European Union will grow above and beyond the expectation of any American administration. It will rise to superpower status and evolve into the most powerful dictatorship that ever existed.

When the dollar officially collapses and we know this crash will happen, and when its effects ripple around the globe, the crisis will provide the Antichrist with the perfect platform to enact solutions that will bring the EU prosperity along with the nations of the world. As US President Obama shaped and instituted policy to help remedy the Great Recession, the Antichrist will do the same, only Scripture tells us that his policies succeed. During America's broken condition, the EU will have opportunity to rise to its forecasted position of the greatest political power to ever have existed. The Antichrist will bring the world back on financial tract and global economies will experience prosperity in the same way that Adolph Hitler brought wealth to Germany in his first few years of power. A writer stated that if Adolph Hitler died three years after gaining the chancellorship in Germany, history would have recorded him as Germany's greatest chancellor. It will be exactly the same with the Antichrist.

Once the Antichrist signs the peace treaty with Israel, about three and a half years afterwards, he places the abomination of desolation in the Jewish Temple. At this time, his evil, diabolical side surfaces and the nations react. The destruction of the EU (Babylon) occurs just before the Battle of Armageddon. Rumors from the east and north trouble the Antichrist. He then sets out to conquer many nations, and he establishes himself in Jerusalem.

A people from the north and a great nation will come to destroy the land of Babylon (Jeremiah 4:6-7, Daniel 11:40, 45). This great nation may be the US, which unites with the Soviet Union to destroy the European Union. Jeremiah reiterates this, and tells us that the great nation is from the farthest parts of the earth (Jer. 6:22). After destroying Babylon (Europe), they come to take Jerusalem, which the Antichrist controls. China follows. Jeremiah 5:15-16 states: "Behold, I will bring a nation against you from afar, 0 house of Israel, says the Lord: it is a mighty nation, it is an ancient nation, a nation whose language you do not know, nor can you understand what they say. Their quiver is like an open tomb, they are all mighty men."

The US position in the world will continue to decline as the EU rises to superpower status. When the EU becomes the final world empire, the US will remain a strong nation, though not a lone superpower. After the dollar's fall, America's prosperity will result from the Antichrist's solutions. The US will endorse EU policy and support the Antichrist until near the end of the Tribulation. When the US discovers the Antichrist's true colors and takes action, the nation will aid in carrying out Biblical prophecy. Fulfilling Babylon's judgment, the US will launch an attack on Europe. From there, the US will join the world's armies at the Battle of Armageddon. The US is a very trusting nation, and places great faith in its allies, especially in Europe. Their ties reach far and go deep. This reliance and the US's weakened position will prevent the US from taking action until it is too late.

A VIEW TO THE PAST

It was American armed forces who claimed the victory at the end of World War II and undertook the task of rebuilding Europe. The Soviet Union, which lay on Western Europe's borders, threatened to spread Communism to the ends of the earth. The Cold War between communism and Western democracy began, and global stability depended heavily on the United States. No country possessed America's combination of military power, wealth, and political authority. The US supplied Europe with the funds to rebuild itself, and even provided for its defense against Communist forces in postwar Europe. The US will never view the EU as a future military threat, or as the potential cause of war and conflict. America will follow the Antichrist blindly, just as the nation has endorsed other dictators throughout its history. In part, its blindness will be a symptom of its own internal problems. A lack of effective US leadership will also be responsible.

Many skeptics view the EU as an economic grouping with too many differences to ever amount to anything politically. Others blinded by the Antichrist himself, will believe in his solutions for the world's ills. The rest will not care about world events while absorbed in their own personal lives, and will have no inkling that God's judgments are about to be unleashed upon the world. By the time America realizes the depravity of the Antichrist and takes action, the armies of the world will be on the road to Armageddon.

15

CONFIRMING THE COVENANT

The European Neighborhood Policy (ENP) is a collective agreement, initiated by the European Union (EU), involving many nations. It has been funded and implemented for a seven-year period (2007-2013). Indications and assurances of the pursuit of peace, between Israel and the Palestinian Authority, and in the Middle East as a whole, are included in the agreement.

THE PEACE TREATY

The Tribulation begins when the Antichrist negotiates a peace treaty with Israel, guaranteeing its security. Three and a half years after these negotiations, he stands in the Jewish Temple and declares himself a god. The Antichrist then lays siege to Jerusalem, and seeks to exterminate the Jews. Zechariah 13:8 tells us that two-thirds of the Jewish population dies due to his exploits. The verse affirms: "And it shall come to pass, in all the land, says the Lord, that two-thirds in it shall be cut off and die; but one-third shall be left in it." The remaining third, God refines. They call upon His name and He hears them. There are 13.3 million Jews worldwide. This would amount to the deaths of over eight million Jewish people in a three-and-a- half-year time period!

Nearly all Bible prophecy centers on Israel, including the prophecies dealing with the Tribulation. Today the Middle East is a primary focus in international affairs. The Center for Contemporary Arab Studies at Georgetown University concluded: "This very quick trip through history shows that, for several millennia, the Middle East was at the very center of the world stage. In the few hundred years between the sixteenth and the twentieth century's, it drifted to the wings. Now it has once again been recalled, by a mysterious providence, to the center ."Bible scholars view the reestablishment of the Israeli nation as the most important sign of the end times, because so much of Bible prophecy centers on Israel.

Many commentators regard Ezekiel 37:1-22, which prophecies about God's bringing the Jews back to their land from the valley of dry bones, as a reference to the restoration that took place in 1948. Ezekiel 37 predicted Israel's rebirth as a nation, and in 1948 this prophecy saw fulfillment. The skeletons in the valley are a picture of the way many Jews appeared after the Holocaust. The bones cry, "our hope is lost." At the moment of their great despair, God brings about this miracle, which is exactly what occurred. The passage discusses God's bringing the Israelites from all of the nations where they lived, to their own land. During the Cold War, Communist nations did not allow Jews who desired to go to Israel to leave their countries. With the fall of the Berlin Wall in 1989, another prophecy saw fulfillment. Ezekiel 36:24 states: "For I will take you from among the nations, and gather you out of all countries, and bring you into your own land."

With the fall of communism, Jews who lived under the oppression of totalitarian regimes returned home. Restrictions on Jewish emigration lifted in the Soviet Union, and twenty thousand immigrants per month poured into Israel. The US, which had always provided open doors to immigrating Jews, decided to limit the number of Soviet Jews entering the country. Israel and some American Zionist organizations pressured the US not to admit them unless strong family links to current residents existed. Some 90 percent of refugees preferred the US to Israel as a destination, but this restriction forced them to go to Israel. Many remained there because of an Israeli requirement for a refund of fares and related costs should such refugees attempt to move to another country. Politics did not force Jews to return to Israel, but God's divine hand brought them into their land.

Although Israel became a nation, it does not possess all the land God promised to Abraham. Under King Solomon, Israel came to possess most of it. The land promised was Palestine, stretching from the Sinai Desert north and east to the Euphrates River. This includes present day Israel, Lebanon, and the West Bank of Jordan, plus substantial portions of Syria, Iraq, and Saudi Arabia.

ISRAEL'S HISTORY OF CONFLICT

- In 1948, Israel became a nation.
- Five Arab countries-Egypt, Jordan, Iraq, Syria, and Lebanon-declared war and attacked the new nation.
- In 1949, Israel signed a series of truces with the Arab countries.
- In 1956, Egyptian President Gamal Abdel Nasser barred Israeli ships from using the Suez Canal. He launched guerrilla attacks against Israel. Israel attacked Egypt and occupied the Sinai Peninsula and the Gaza strip.
- In 1957, Israel withdrew from these territories under strong pressure from the UN, US, and Soviet Union.
- In 1964, in Cairo, at an Arab League meeting, activists formed the Palestinian Liberation Organization.

- In 1967, after a marked rise in activities against Israel by the Arab countries, Israel launched a preemptive strike. The Israelis destroyed the Egyptian Air Force on the ground. Israeli troops swept to the banks of the Suez Canal, and fought the Syrians in the Golan Heights. Jordan entered the war. When the armies declared a cease-fire, the Israeli army occupied the Sinai Peninsula and Gaza strip, East Jerusalem, the West Bank, and the Golan Heights. Israel absorbed East Jerusalem in 1967.

Theologian and author John Walvoord commented concerning Israel's victories in this war: As a result of the war, Israel increased her territory from eight thousand to thirty-four thousand square miles and doubled her population. Most important from the prophetic point of view, Jerusalem was back in the hands of Israel. The prospect of another war averted for the time being. Israel had suffered less than a thousand battle fatalities in contrast to thirty thousand Arab dead. Israel had tremendously increased her stature as a nation among nations and left the military might of her enemies in shambles. The world had begun to notice the prophets' predictions that the Jews will "never again...be uprooted from the land I have given them (Amos 9:15).

- The UN Security Council adopted resolution 242, which calls for Israeli withdrawal from "territories occupied" in the June War. It also calls for Arab recognition of Israel's "right to live in peace within secure and recognized boundaries." The United Nations invited the PLO to take part in a General Assembly discussion of the Palestine question. It approved a resolution recognizing the right of the Palestinian people to independence and sovereignty, and gave the PLO observer status at its sessions. The Arab League endorsed the PLO as the "sole legitimate representative of the Palestinian people."
- In 1970, PLO guerrillas from Jordan made raids on Jerusalem. President Nasser died, and Anwar el- Sadat succeeded him.
- In 1973, Egyptian and Syrian forces attacked Israel on Yom Kippur. A Soviet- and American-sponsored cease-fire resolution ended the fighting and led to an international peace conference at Geneva.
- In 1974, Israel and Egypt signed a disengagement agreement, and Israel signed a similar one for the withdrawal of its forces from Syria and from part of the Golan Heights.
- In 1975, Israel signed a second disengagement treaty with Egypt. In that year the General Assembly adopted a resolution denouncing Zionism "as a form of racism and racial discrimination." The move outraged Israel and its supporters.
- Menachem Begin became Prime Minister of Israel. President Sadat of Egypt went to Jerusalem. This marked the first visit by an Arab head of state to Israel.
- In 1978, the top leaders of Israel, Egypt, and the US met at Camp David for twelve days and agreed on two bases for Middle East peace. In 1979, these leaders signed the Camp David Peace Treaty.
- In 1982, Israeli forces invaded southern Lebanon with the goal of ousting the PLO. They besieged Beirut for ten weeks, and sent in American troops. The next year, Ronald Reagan sent Secretary of State George Shultz to the Middle East to conclude an accord on the withdrawal of

all foreign troops from Lebanon. Israel and Lebanon signed the agreement. King Hussein of Jordan and Yasir Arafat of the PLO agreed on an initiative that called for an international peace conference under United Nations auspices. The initiative foundered because the two sides could not agree on how to include the Palestinians, and because Mr. Arafat refused to accept United States participation.

THE PEACE PROCESS

In 1991, after the Gulf War, former President Bush sent Secretary of State James Baker on a series of trips to the region to explore compromises that would begin the Arab/Israeli peace process. Israel and Lebanon would discuss the future of Israel's declared "security zone" in southern Lebanon, which Israel had held since 1982. Syria would promise peace in exchange for the Golan Heights, captured by Israel in the 1967 Middle East War. Israel and Jordan would find a solution to the twenty-four-year Israeli occupation of the West Bank of the Jordan River, territory that Israel seized from Jordan in the 1967 war. Former King Hussein formally renounced his claim to the territory in 1988, clearing the way for a Palestinian state there. Sixty percent of Jordan's population is Palestinian.

The major dispute is between Israel and the Palestinians. Palestinians in the West Bank and Gaza Strip seek autonomy over their affairs, in the form of Arab elections in the occupied territories, independent Palestinian municipal governments, and Palestinian administration of police forces, schools, and health care centers. Palestinians say the Arab eastern half of the city should be their capital. Israelis adamantly oppose negotiations over Jerusalem.

THE OSLO ACCORDS

In 1993, Israeli and Palestinian delegations secretly negotiated in Oslo, Norway. They signed the Oslo accords at a Washington ceremony on September 13, 1993, during which former Palestinian leader Yasser Arafat and Israeli Prime Minister Yitzhak Rabin shook hands, ending decades as sworn enemies. The Israelis and Palestinians recognized each other's mutual political rights, and agreed to strive to live in peaceful coexistence. They set up a time table in which Israeli troops would withdraw from Gaza and Jericho, and for Palestinians would set up their own government. They looked to 1999 for the finalization of a permanent settlement.

Despite Israel's special thirty-year relationship with the US, Israel met secretly in Oslo, Norway, for this historic conference with Palestine. They notified the US barely a few days before its finalization. US Secretary of State Warren Christopher first viewed the "Declaration of Principles" in an Israeli newspaper. Israeli Political commentator Daniel Ben-Simon stated that "the Oslo agreement put Israel's patron to shame."

On September 28, 1995, at a White House ceremony, Israelis and Palestinians signed another deal known as the "Interim Agreement," or "Oslo 2." The four-hundred-page pact allowed for a second stage of autonomy for the Palestinians, giving them self-rule in various Arab cities and villages while allowing guarded settlements to remain. The Oslo Accords have not gone according to plan. The continual conflicts that have arisen between the Israelis and Palestinians have caused the peace process to reach many impasses. Former President Clinton sent former Secretary of State Warren Christopher to the region for talks. Madeline Albright followed in his footsteps. The European Union has sent several delegations to the area. Still the peace process has barely moved along.

On September 28, 2000, Israeli opposition leader Ariel Sharon led a delegation on a visit to the Temple Mount for a message of peace. After his visit, crowds of Palestinians in Gaza and the West Bank attacked Israeli security forces with guns and rocks. Palestinians blamed Sharon's visit to the Muslim holy site for sparking the conflict, which continued into 2001 with each side blaming the other.

In July of 2000, Bill Clinton, Ehud Barak, and Yasser Arafat met at Camp David to work out the final arrangements for a Palestinian state. Barak made concessions above and beyond the framework of Oslo. He offered the Palestinians control over a large portion of Jerusalem, but Arafat walked away without making any counter-proposals. Both sides did not demonstrate flexibility during the summit to negotiate a settlement. When it became clear to the Palestinian authority that Israel could not fulfill every demand of the necessary reciprocal compromises, the Palestinian Authority chose to break off negotiations without offering any of its own proposals. Clinton placed the blame for the failure of the talks squarely at Arafat's feet.

Israel transferred virtually every Arab City and town in the territories to Arafat's control, supplied the Arab militia with weapons, began paying Arafat a multi-million-dollar monthly allowance, and lobbied for additional financial support to permit the Palestinian authority to build an airport, operate radio and television networks, and deal with other countries as a sovereign power. But the terror and violence accelerated. The Israeli death toll soared, and captured documents proved that Arafat and his Palestinian authority schemed with terrorist states such as Iran and Syria to acquire armaments and fund terrorism. Their aim remains the same-the destruction of Israel. Again, at the Taba Talks in January 2001, Israel once again showed its willingness to make far-reaching political and strategic compromises in order to achieve peace.

In February 2001, Sharon defeated Ehud Barak for the position of Prime Minister. In December 2002, Sharon made a speech at the Herzliya Conference Institute of Policy and Strategy, and stated that the next phase cannot continue until there is a calm from terrorism and until the Palestinian government reforms, that peace cannot occur with Arafat as president of the Palestinian Authority, nor without the dismantling of all existing security bodies, the majority of which are involved in terror. In 2004 Yasser Arafat died.

THE EUROPEAN UNION AND ISRAEL

For the Tribulation to begin, the European Union must sign a treaty with Israel, guaranteeing Israel's peace. The US sponsors the current peace initiative. Henry Kissinger suggested in late November of 1990 that US leadership in the Middle East might be ending.

"We are in a transitional period.....I would think that over a period of ten years, many of the security responsibilities that the United States is now shouldering in the Gulf ought to be carried by the Europeans who receive a larger share of the oil from the region."

For many years, the EU has followed developments in the Middle East closely, particularly the Arab-

Israeli dispute. Only since the late 1970s has the EU taken a common West European stand on the Arab-Israeli conflict. They support a peaceful solution based on the 1980 Venice declaration. It affirms the right of all states in the region, including Israel, to exist within secure frontiers, and the right of the Palestinian people to self-determination. The Union believes an international peace conference on the Middle East would provide the most suitable framework for negotiations and provides aid and economic assistance to the territories. It is now an EU plan to become a leading player in the Middle East. Garret Fitzgerald stated in his report to the Trilateral Commission on the Israeli-Palestinian issue: "In some European capitals, where there has for a long time been a feeling that Europe's interest in the Middle East is greater than that of the United States but where the United States' much greater influence in the region is recognized albeit with some sense of frustration, this American approach has been criticized as too limited and narrow, and also as being too optimistic....If, however, the policy fails, many in Europe would wish to see their governments in the European Union taking up the torch, without, perhaps, having a very clear idea as to how they could succeed where the United States had failed"

In a statement by the EU Presidency to a joint meeting of members of the European Parliament and the Knesset on January 17, 1990, EU diplomats made it clear that if the Baker initiative failed: "The Twelve will be active in seeking an alternative to the Israeli-Palestinian dialogue as a means of advancing the kind of settlement advocated by the ED." The EU feels qualified to play an important role in the advancement of peace, security and development in the Middle East, both by reason of its geographic proximity and its long-standing ties with the region. The Union regards itself as the most important economic group in the world today, with corresponding political influence. It also provides two of the permanent members of the UN Security Council.

The Mediterranean area is the Union's third main market for Community products, and the source from which the Union obtains some of its basic needs. On the EU's current agenda of foreign policy aims is "to play a very active part in efforts to achieve a lasting peace and stability in the Middle East."

On the day the fighting ended in the Gulf, Luxembourg Foreign Minister Jacques Poos declared that the EU must help to establish peace and security in the Middle East. EU foreign ministers discussed the challenge of promoting stability in the Middle East after the war, hoping to play an influential role in rebuilding the region. Poos said in an interview that "the Middle East needs a Marshall Plan-a Europe and, if possible, worldwide plan." The foreign ministers have underlined their willingness to do everything possible to ensure lasting peace in the region.

At a meeting in Luxembourg, EU members pleaded with then US Secretary of State James Baker for a role in the peace process. The European request evoked a lukewarm response. He suggested that the EU have observer status. During an emergency meeting the EU expressed fears that Washington will sideline the Union. They issued a statement to the New York Times in 1992, in which they stated that they "hoped for a full role as cosponsor of any Middle East peace conference. Israel stated that it wants the EU to have only observer status at any peace talks. It has long been concerned over the EU's contacts with the Palestine Liberation Organization. One EU aide, however, noted that [the EU] would have to live with the peace, and wants to be part of the creation of it." He added that it firmly believed that "the more international the conference, the better its chances." Israel fears that the EU, which has proclaimed the need for Palestinian self-determination, has a strong pro- Palestinian and pro-Arab bias.

EU Middle East experts say the Union can make a "positive contribution" to the peace talks through its close historical, political, and economic links with the Arab world. The EU used political and economic pressure to persuade Israel to invite the Union to the negotiating table. Several EU ministers insisted that Union aid for Israel-and the Arab countries-depended on a heightened EU role in the Middle East. EU diplomats admitted that in Israel's case, the trade and economic argument was probably more effective. The EU is Israel's leading trading partner; the EU is Israel's largest market for exports and its second largest source of imports after the US. EU ministers promised Israel a closer economic relationship with the EU. They offered it on the condition that Israel recognizes the Union's hopes of playing a "special role" in the Middle East. Of all the EU states, the Netherlands is an especially keen defender of Israel's political and economic interests. According to former Italian Prime Minister Gianni de Michelis:

"We insisted on being among the countries promoting the conference, on equal footing with the United States and the Soviet Union. We would find it difficult, if not unfathomable, to accept a lesser role, considering the contribution the Twelve can make to the peace process and to subsequent developments. We wish to be present not because we are seeking prestige, but because of the clear advantages our presence would bring to everyone. We have explained this several times to our Israeli friends who up until now have been those most reluctant to accept the Europeans, whom they consider as favoring the Arabs and thus wanting to transform the future conference into a court against Israel... However, vital its tie to the United States may be, the one to Europe is perhaps even more so in the long term. Israel is the daughter of Europe's history, and not only of the holocaust that was a tragedy not only for the Jews, but also for Europe....Anchoring Israel to Europe means eliminating one of Israel's motives for insecurity, that of having to rely on an ally that is geographically distant, not only in terms of military assistance but also in terms of development"

The EU believes it can play an important role in the peace process by providing Israelis and Arabs with economic incentives to reach a diplomatic solution. They have begun work on a regional Arab-Israeli economic cooperation program. The EU will aim at the creation of new and binding trade, industrial, and environmental links between Israel, the Palestinians, and all Arab countries in the region. The EU's Middle East experts underline that "a precise program for cooperation, the economic advantages clearly spelt out, would be an added incentive to finding a solution to all political problems."

Former Italian Prime Minister Gianni de Michelis and Former French Foreign Minister Roland Dumas met in Sicily along with the Middle East ambassadors. They called for "a renewed, dynamic role" for Europe, including a seat at the negotiating table. At a press conference, Dumas said Europe must take on the role the Soviet Union could no longer play. It was no good asking Europe to make a major economic contribution while virtually excluding it from the key questions of disarmament and regional security.

CONFERENCE ON SECURITY AND COOPERATION IN THE MIDDLE EAST

The EU bases its Middle East proposals on the Conference on Security and Cooperation in the Middle East. This proposal, issued in 1990 by the foreign ministries of Italy and Spain, is a regional arrangement for the Middle East. It takes in the Arab world, Israel, and Iran. The CSCE's global approach promotes peace in the Middle East. It acts as a multilateral forum covering the entire region. Agreed on will be guidelines on several issues: security, economic development, water and other natural resources, environmental issues, and human rights.

The Conference on Security and Cooperation in the Mediterranean and the Middle East reserves a special role for the UN. Participants include the US, Soviet Union, the EU and some of its member countries, and other states from Morocco to Iran. The euro-Mediterranean conference met for the first time in Barcelona in 1995. It marked the first time foreign ministers from Syria and Israel attended the same conference.

The EU took a lead role by pledging more aid to Gaza and the West Bank than the US. It is at work creating a free trade zone with Israel. The conference launched the euro-Mediterranean Partnership and established the euro-Mediterranean Free Trade Area.

MEDIA INSIGHT (GLOBAL WATCH 16TH DECEMBER 2011
THE BARCELONA PROCESS (EUROMED)

Union for the Mediterranean (UfM) previously known as Euromed was a multilateral partnership that encompassed 43 countries from Europe and the Mediterranean Basin: the 27 member states of the European Union and 16 Mediterranean partner countries from North Africa, the Middle East and the Balkans. It was created in July 2008 as a re-launched Euro-Mediterranean Partnership (the Barcelona Process), when a plan to create an autonomous Mediterranean Union was dropped. The Union had the aim of promoting stability and prosperity throughout the Mediterranean region. Nevertheless, its 2009 and 2010 Summits could not be held due to the stalemate of the Arab-Israeli peace process after the Gaza war. It has now been superseded by the European Neighborhood Policy (ENP).

THE PRINCIPLES OF THE MEDITERRANEAN UNION

The Union for the Mediterranean introduced new institutions into the Euro-Mediterranean Partnership with the aim of increasing its visibility such as the creation of a Secretariat.

The commercial connections between the European countries and the African ones are very important. They have created the premises for a future economic union between the Mediterranean non-European states and the communitarian countries.

The Mediterranean Union reunites countries from Europe, Middle East. and North Africa countries that have access to the Mediterranean Sea, forming an economic community by taking the model of the early European Union.

As it would be formed by the E.U. states and the Mediterranean countries, the Mediterranean Union would have a State President Council, an executive council, ministerial councils, a Permanent Commission that would act like a Secretary Department, a consolidated Parliament reunion and its own bank. Such an organization could have a big role in the area in solving diverse problems, form ecological issues to immigration

From the European Union side: the 27 European Union member states (Austria, Belgium, Bulgaria, Cyprus, Czech Republic, Denmark, Estonia, Finland, France, Germany, Greece, Hungary, Ireland, Italy, Latvia, Lithuania, Luxembourg, Malta,

Netherlands, Poland, Portugal, Romania, Slovakia, Slovenia, Spain, Sweden and United Kingdom.)

From the side of the Mediterranean Partner countries: Albania, Algeria, Bosnia and Herzegovina, Croatia, Egypt, Israel, Jordan, Lebanon, Mauritania, Monaco, Montenegro, Morocco, the Palestinian Authority, Syria (self-suspended on 22 June 2011), Tunisia and Turkey. Libya as an observer state.

MEDIA INSIGHT (GLOBAL WATCH 16TH DECEMBER 2011) THE BARCELONA PROCESS (EUROMED)

Even though the Antichrist is not called the King of the West we can make the assumption that the empire from which he will come to prominence will be from the west of Israel since the power blocks which come against him in Israel will be from the north, south and east.

An interesting perspective to be observed is that if the ten toes of the image in Nebuchadnezzar's (Daniel 2) are in reference to the emergence of a Revival of the Roman Empire ...which many believe that the European Union will fulfill, then it is interesting here that Daniel states in Daniel 11:43 that the Antichrist will conquer the northern and Egyptian attack and then extend his military rule beyond Egypt into Africa.

If one was to see the boundaries of ancient Rome at the time of Christ and 100 years after, one would see that the Roman Empire's geographical power had fully extended across past Egypt across the whole of North Africa capturing the whole of the Mediterranean basin. It would seem according to scripture that the latter day Roman Empire will seek to duplicate a geographical stranglehold that will mirror exactly that as over 2000 years ago.

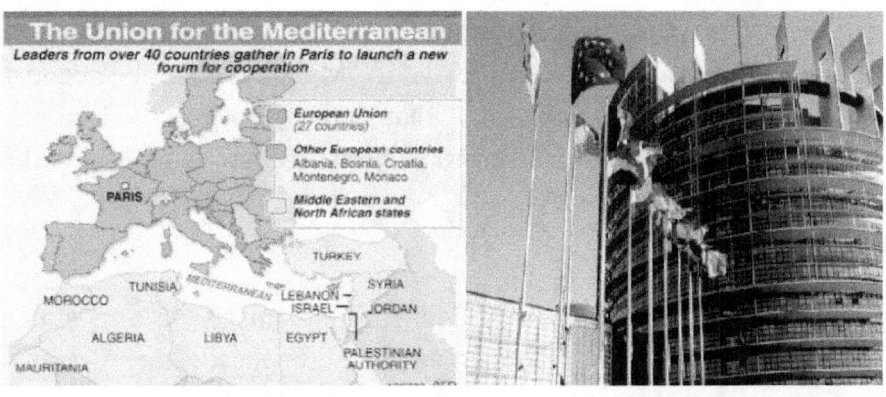

Furthermore it is of great significance that Europe is now using France to spearhead the Mediterranean initiative to bring the nations of the Middle East and North Africa into a close economic relationship with the European Union. Could this all be embryonic steps of Europe's attempts dominate the nerve center of the world before deciding to fully conquer these territories through military subjugation when they begin to rebel against the Antichrist rule.

The EU took a leading role in the first Palestinian elections. They coordinated an international observation operation to ensure their success. The Union voiced anger at Washington shutting it out of an emergency summit held in Washington in 1996. The French foreign minister's spokesman stated that "the European Union has its place in the peace process. It is bound to be part of a peace settlement because it finances 75 percent of aid to the Palestinian territories." To establish its role, the Union invited Arafat to meet its foreign ministries before he went to Washington. Italy's foreign minister stated: "Tonight's meeting of the European troika with President Arafat in Luxembourg underlines the role of Europe in the Middle East peace process, especially since it is being held before the Washington Summit." The EU several occasions voiced its anger over giving its dollars without having any say in the region. They desired a role alongside the United States. Shireen Hunter, visiting research fellow at the Brussels-based Centre for European Policy Studies, stated: "If Europe is going to have any reality whatsoever, Europe has to act in one of the most important strategic areas otherwise Europe can't be taken seriously as a global actor." Europe continues to press for a greater role in the region, voicing its desire to have a political role as strong as its economic one.

The Palestinians and Arab countries have been pushing for a greater European role to counter what they see as Washington's pro-Israeli stance. The Union is convinced that peace in the Middle East depends on the full implementation of the existing agreement between Israel and the Palestinians. They also believe in a final solution based on international law as set by the United Nations and the principle of land-for-peace. The Union calls for "total withdrawal for total security."

The European Parliament stated that the Union "cannot nor should not, accept East Jerusalem to be considered part of the territory and sovereignty of Israel." The Union urges the option of a Palestinian state and they refer to east Jerusalem as a Palestinian city. The Union wrote former President Clinton to propose a joint American-European initiative to revive the Middle East peace negotiations. The United States politely brushed off the European proposal. Although the US welcomed European efforts and said they had a productive role to play, the US reaffirmed its position as having the central role in the Middle East peace negotiations.

Europe essentially put its foot in the door of Middle East diplomacy. At a meeting of European and Mediterranean foreign ministers, the Dutch foreign minister brought together Vasser Arafat and Israel's foreign minister on the sidelines of the conference. The EU president exclaimed, "it's indispensable, the political role of Europe here." He was speaking of the euro-Mediterranean forum. In the Amsterdam Treaty negotiated in the Summer of 1997, the Union called for and committed itself to peace in the Middle East. European diplomats hoped to get the two men together again at the next Euro-Med meeting, to win a greater role in the Mideast Peace Process.

In early 1998, the EU Commission urged the European Union to review its aid program to the Middle East peace process, demanding concessions from Israel and a bigger say in the US led negotiations. In the policy paper, the Commission said that the EU should insist that Israel stop sealing off Palestinian territories from the outside world. It noted that living conditions deteriorated despite the mounds of money the EU dumped into the region. The paper said the EU should insist on participating alongside the United States in all talks between Israel and the Palestinians, and should take the lead in coordinating international economic aid. The Commissioner responsible for Middle East policy stated: "We think it is perfectly logical, as may happen in a private company if you are the main shareholder. It wouldn't be normal for you not to be included on the board."

Since 1998, the EU's aggressive determination to be part of the peace process helped to evolve its role as a "key player in the political and economic process." The EU's recent stated position on the Middle East peace process is that of a "promoter of a comprehensive, just and lasting peace and of prosperity for the region."

The EU also acts as a "facilitator in the peace process." It holds regular meetings with the main actors involved. The EU Troika (present and incoming Presidency, the High Representative for CFSP, and the Commission) make routine visits to the Near East. The activities of the EU Special Envoy for the Peace Process, the political talks with all parties, aimed at promoting the EU's positions, contribute to strengthen the role of the Union in the negotiations for the final settlement of the Israeli-Arab conflict.

The EU presidency issues frequent statements concerning the various stalemates that have occurred in the peace process. They also have partaken in monitoring the early Palestinian elections of 1996 and the training of Palestinian policeman. The EU has also teamed up with the US, as agreed in the Trans-Atlantic Declaration, to work together in the peace process. At the US-EU summit in Washington on December 18, 1998, the EU stated in their Declaration on the Middle East Peace Process: We will work together, including through our respective envoys, in the political and economic area, to build on this achievement and to help the parties move the peace process forward to a successful conclusion. We will use our partnership to support the implementation of seek ways to help the parties in the Lebanese and Syrian tracks to restart negotiations with the aim of reaching a comprehensive settlement.

The EU lends a good deal of economic support to the Middle East region. They are the largest donor of non-military aid to the peace process. The EU is the first donor of financial and technical assistance to the Palestinian authority. They are the first trading partner and a major economic, scientific and research partner of Israel, and are also a major partner of Lebanon, Syria, Jordan, and Egypt. In 2000, they signed the EU-Israel Association Agreement and committed themselves to establishing a partnership which provides for close political and mutually beneficial trade and investment relations together with economic, social, financial, civil scientific, technological and cultural cooperation.

In the Laeken Declaration, which resulted from the European Council's meeting in Laeken on December 14 and 15, 2001, EU leaders issued a "Declaration on the Situation in the Middle East," stating that "it is imperative to put an end to violence." The EU reaffirms Israel's right to live in peace and security, and supports the establishment of a Palestinian State. The EU appeals to the Palestinian authority to end terrorism, and demands that they dismantle the Hamas' and Islamic Jilhad's terrorist networks, "including the arrest and prosecution of all suspects: a public appeal in Arabic for an end to the armed intifada." The EU demands that the Israeli government withdraw all military forces, and lift all closures and restrictions-including freezes on settlements and operations-directed against Palestinian infrastructures.

A key statement of interest to students of prophecy reads: "The European Union remains convinced that setting up a third party monitoring mechanism would serve the interests of both parties. It is prepared to play an active role in such a mechanism." Could this lead to the guarantee of peace in the region and the Covenant of Death?

In May of 2002, when President George Bush, Jr. met with Commission President Prodi during a summit, he affirmed the EU's importance in the Middle East Peace process by stating: "The United States and the EU share a common vision of two states, Palestine and Israel, living side by side in peace and security. This vision offers the Palestinian people a new opportunity to choose how they live. We should take this opportunity to help build institutions that will serve the Palestinian people, a Palestinian state and its neighbors, as well....The EU, as well and the United States has an important role to play. When the EU and the United States work together we multiply our effectiveness"

In the July 2002 issue of The Federalist, Guido Montani, the Secretary General of the UEF in Italy, stated: "Presently the European Union does not have the means necessary for intervening adequately in the Middle East. The Federalists therefore are calling on the Union's governments to convene urgently a meeting of the European Council and to declare a State of Emergency, granting the European Commission all the military and budgetary powers for solving the crisis in the Middle East" He adds that the European Commission will act as a "provincial European government," which should call for an international conference. He refers to "The European Peace Plan," which must call for "the immediate creation of a Palestinian State." Mr. Montani also adds that "the European Union, unlike the USA and Russia, has an interest in proposing to all of the Middle East countries (and not just to Palestine) a Marshall plan for development and peace."

In August 2002, the Danish presidency of the European Union announced that it was working on a three- stage Middle East peace plan, which envisioned the creation of an independent Palestinian state in 2005. The Danish plan hoped to signal to the Arab world that Europe is still a major player in the Middle East region. Former Danish president Per Stig Moeller stated: "We must make progress on security, political and economic issues to strengthen the belief among Palestinians in a state that will be theirs and that is within reach, and reassure Israelis that they will at last have security within their own borders."

Thus the groundwork for the treaty spoken of in Scriptures exists and only awaits the arrival of the Antichrist to formalize and sign it, yet the events still continue to evolve. In December 2002, the EU, US, UN, and Russia held a Quartet meeting to discuss Middle East peace, and put forth a road map that envisions two states, Israel and Palestine, living side by side in peace and security.

On Apr. 30, 2003, the Roadmap for Peace took place based upon a speech by President Bush and the principles of the Oslo Accords. This plan is supervised by the Quartet: the United States, the European Union, the Russian Federation and the United Nations. It called for serious alterations in the Palestinian government and resulted in the appointment of Palestinian Authority Prime Minister Mahmoud Abbas. Afterward a summit took place with Sharon and Abbas reaffirming their commitment to the Roadmap. Sharon promised withdrawal of Israeli troops from Palestinian areas, and Abbas pledged an end to the Intifada and the Palestinian culture of hate against Israel. Despite the agreement, Palestinian terrorists carried out a suicide bombing in Jerusalem and the Israeli Cabinet waged war against Hamas and other terrorist groups, and halted the diplomatic process.

Later that year at the Fourth Herzliya Conference, Prime Minister Sharon presented a plan for Israel's unilateral disengagement from the Gaza Strip and northern Samaria in exchange for peace. The disengagement plan, called for evacuating nearly 9,000 Israeli residents living in Gaza and the West Bank.

In 2005, at the Sharm el-Sheikh Summit I, Sharon met with PA President Abbas, Egyptian President Hosni Mubarak and King Abdullah of Jordan to announce the implementation of Israel's disengagement from the Gaza Strip and parts of the West Bank. Abbas and Sharon agreed upon a Ceasefire. Later in August Israel pulled all of its citizens out of the Gaza Strip and the Northern West Bank.

In 2007, Israeli Prime Minister Ehud Olmert's accepted the revised Arab Peace Initiative. In response to the March 28, 2007 Arab League Summit at Riyadh, Olmert invited the Arab heads of state to a meeting in Israel to further discuss the initiative and collaborate on improving it. Olmert met with Abbas, Mubarak and Jordan's King Abdullah II. They discussed containment of Hamas in the Gaza Strip and to strengthen Abbas' Fatah party in the West Bank. Later that year, Israeli Prime Minister Ehud Olmert and

Palestinian Authority President Mahmoud Abbas signed a joint statement in Annapolis, Md. to lay the groundwork for peace talks.

In 2008, President Bush embarked on a tour of a number of Middle East countries, starting with Israel. The purpose of the visit was to advance peace negotiations initiated at the Annapolis conference in Nov. 2007. Bush urged the Palestinian side to dismantle the terrorist infrastructure and also called on Israel to halt settlement construction and remove unauthorized settler outposts.

The Peace Valley plan is an effort personally supported by Israeli President Shimon Peres, which seeks to promote a new approach based on economic cooperation, and promotion of joint economic and business projects. In May 2008, Tony Blair, the special envoy for the Quartet announced a new plan for peace and for Palestinian rights, based heavily on the ideas of the Peace Valley plan.

In December 2008, the EU expressed the hope that Lebanon - Israel peace talks would be possible. The EU has praised the Arab Peace Initiative, as a major step forward for the Middle East Peace Process, since it offers a basis for peaceful and normalized relations between Israel and all 22 members of the Arab League.

In 2013 the resolution of the Arab-Israeli conflict is now a strategic priority for Europe. They believe that without this peace, there will be little chance of dealing with other problems in the Middle East. The EU's objective is a two-state solution with an independent, democratic, viable Palestinian state living side-by- side with Israel and its other neighbors.

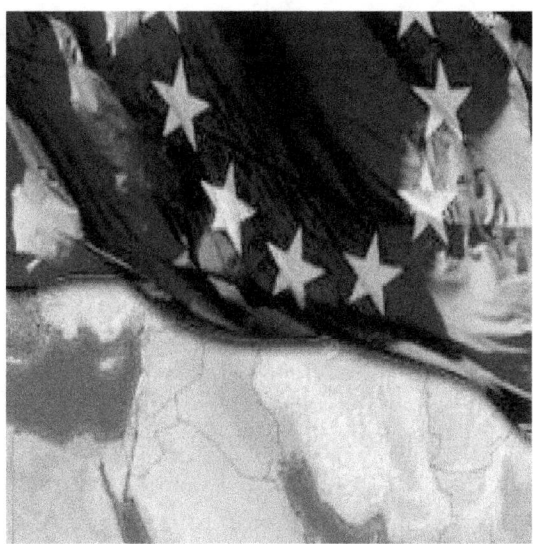

The Bible tells us that the Antichrist confirms the covenant with Israel, and guarantees Israel's peace. In 1993, the Federalist Trust, a European think-tank organization that aids in formulating EU policy, and is ahead of its time usually suggesting policy that the EU adopts a few decades later, published a report on the Middle East. They wrote up a proposed treaty that guarantees Israel's peace. The proposal offers the security that the US initiative fails to offer. The report proposes the establishment of a "regional security community" as the basis for the Arab-Israeli peace settlement. The proposed treaty states that the guarantor states would protect the community against external attacks. The Union would secure Israel's peace with its army. The Scriptures state that the Antichrist confirms the covenant with many. The proposed treaty includes the world's great powers and reads:

Moreover, the incorporation of the great powers into the security package as both the guarantors and supervisors of this arrangement raises the costs of violation dramatically. Should a certain state decide to defy the superpowers (and the other co-signatories to the agreement) and to embark on a belligerent/irredentist course, it will clearly identify itself as an aggressor and will run the risk of losing the political goodwill as well as the economic and military support of the international community, thereby dooming such a move. Hence, a security community consisting of a militarily constrained Palestinian state and a demilitarized Golan, guaranteed and strictly supervised by the great powers may satisfy Israel's security concerns and ally its apprehensions of the adverse implications of loosening of the US- Israeli strategic relationship, caused by such a proposed arrangement.

It is likely that this proposed treaty is "the covenant of death" spoken of in Scripture. According to Amos Perlmutter: "People who live in a constant state of war naturally yearn for peace; for a nation, security is the equivalent of sanity for an individual. The Israelis search for security is an obsession, a quest for an almost metaphysical security, even if they know that such protection is beyond their political and military capabilities."

When the Antichrist signs the peace treaty with Israel, this covenant assures Israel total peace. The Israelis will feel safe from the threats of their neighbors. The CSCM is the skeletal form of the proposals yet to come. The EU will guarantee Israel's peace in the region and will act as her protector. The world will view it as one more event in history, no cause for concern. This covenant marks the beginning of the Tribulation and ends the dispensation of grace. With events occurring at unprecedented speed, anything is possible and leaders can sign a treaty almost overnight. According to The European Journal of Internal Affairs:

"Disarmament creates a fourth paradox. Never before has history seen such acceleration. There was a time when governments determined their security priorities on a long-term basis and when diplomats negotiated for many years the finer details of acts, verification, ceilings and the like. Those items seem well and truly passed. Today, diplomats are called upon to establish treaties within six months or a year (as was said by President Bush at the Brussels summit last May), whereas the negotiating process, though working at maximum speed, will nevertheless still be unable to keep pace with the political changes which are speedily occurring both East as in the West"

In Israel's ancient past the nation became part of the empire that took it over. Thus, Israel was Assyria, Babylon, Persia and Rome. Israel will also be part of the EU. Coincidentally Israel voiced a desire to join the European Union and the Union considers Israel a possible candidate country. If the country joined it will have the security of the EU and its territory will belong to the empire. According to Michael Sctender- Auerbach from the think-tank the Century Foundation:

"For Israel, ED membership would not only provide a strong security guarantee, but would afford them all of the economic advantages of the vast ED market. For the security establishment, it could possibly mean even opening the door to membership in NATO. The ED and Israel already have a formal Cooperation Agreement-ratified five years ago by the Knesset, Israel's parliament-and this relationship has influenced economic, political and cultural exchanged"

Auerbach pointed out that Israel joined the Euro-Mediterranean zone, which will boost Israel's financial gains in the textile industry. For Israel to gain entry into the EU it will need to negotiate a peace settlement with the Palestinians consistent with Security Council resolution 242 and to settle its border disputes with Syria and the Golan. He also added that "as an EU member at peace with its neighbors, Israel would bolster Europe's status as a world leader and international power broker. This will also provide Israel with the security and membership in a community of nations that accept and protect them." He added that "the ED can currently guarantee peace without Israel becoming a member of the ED, but Israel as a member will no doubt solidify any peace agreed by providing the same protection as it would for the rest of the Member States." For the first time in history, geopolitical speak now matches what the Scriptures predicted.

THE EUROPEAN NEIGBHOURHOOD POLICY

The European Neighborhood Policy (ENP) is a collective agreement, initiated by the European Union (EU), involving many nations. It has been funded and implemented for a seven-year period (2007-2013). The ENP framework is proposed to the 16 of EU's closest neighbors - Algeria, Armenia, Azerbaijan, Belarus, Egypt, Georgia, Israel, Jordan, Lebanon, Libya, Moldova, Morocco, Palestine, Syria, Tunisia and Ukraine.

The ENP is chiefly a bilateral policy between the EU and each partner country. It is further enriched and complemented by regional and multilateral co-operation initiatives: the Eastern Partnership (launched in Prague in May 2009), the Union for the Mediterranean (the Euro-Mediterranean Partnership, formerly known as the Barcelona Process, re-launched in Paris in July 2008), and the Black Sea Synergy (launched in Kiev in February 2008). Indications and assurances of the pursuit of peace, between Israel and the Palestinian Authority, and in the Middle East as a whole, are included in the agreement.

"For Israel and the Palestinian authority, the Neighborhood Policy is a concrete sign of the EU's engagement. ... Israel has never been willing to make such commitments in writing to any other partner" (Brussels, 9 December 2004).

"The EU-Israel ENP Action Plan opened up new possibilities for developing EU-Israel relations by setting out a wide range of areas for greater cooperation including: promoting peace in the Middle East" (The European Neighborhood Policy Fiches on Partners, December 2006).

Officially, the ENP went into effect on 1 January 2007. Technically, though, the European Neighborhood Policy was finalized in October 2006. Following years of planning, on 17 October 2006, more than €11 billion was allocated to fund the ENP. This was achieved via the European Neighborhood and Partnership Instrument (ENPI), specifically for a span of seven years: 2007-2013. A week later, on 24 October 2006, "general provisions establishing a European Neighborhood and Partnership Interest" were laid down for the same (seven-year) period: 2007 through 2013.

In spite of its good intentions, the Barcelona Process (EuroMed) largely was unsuccessful in its efforts to attain solidarity and peace for all involved. The European Neighborhood Policy was considered to be a confirmation or strengthening of the Euro-Mediterranean Partnership. The ENP fully complements EuroMed and is a manifest fulfillment of its long-term goals, in a seven-year time frame.

In a frequently asked questions (FAQ) section of the European Neighborhood Policy website, the following is stated: "The European Neighborhood Policy (ENP) and the Euro-Mediterranean Partnership (the so-called "Barcelona Process") share the same basis, i.e. bilateral Association Agreements with countries in the region. Both policies make use of the institutions established under those Agreements, allowing for a formal dialogue at various levels. With many goals in common, the Euro-Mediterranean Partnership pursues a multilateral track whereas the ENP provides additional focus and impact through a bilateral approach of mutual commitments to implement reforms and modernization conducive to closer economic integration and political cooperation. ... It [the ENP] is therefore a valuable complement to the Euro-Mediterranean Partnership as it allows each country to develop closer links with the EU, based on its particular needs and capacities.

The Lisbon Treaty commits the EU to the "development of a special relationship with neighboring countries in Eastern Europe, South Caucasus and the South shore of the Mediterranean aiming to establish an area of prosperity and good neighborliness, founded on the values of the Union and characterized by close and peaceful relations based on cooperation".

ISRAEL'S COVENANT OF DEATH

Because the EU holds strong relations with the Arab world, the Antichrist will also use these relations to guarantee Israeli peace. He will campaign for peace in Israel and the region as a whole. Israel will trust him and feel secured by his promises. With him they will sign what the Bible calls their covenant with death. Concerning Israel's signing this agreement, in several places in Scripture the Bible elaborates on the deceit behind this promise. In the book of Isaiah, God reveals the truth of this covenant. Isaiah 28:15, 18 reads: "Because you have said, We have made a covenant with death, and with Sheol we are in agreement: when the overflowing scourge passes through, it will not come to us; for we have made lies our refuge, and under falsehood we have hidden ourselves. Your covenant with death will be annulled, and your agreement with Sheol will not stand; when the overflowing scourge passes through, then you will be trampled down by it"

God is telling the Jewish nation that "with hell they are in agreement" because the man they are dealing with is none other than the Devil in a man's body. The phrase "we have made lies our refuge" exposes that the guarantees of the treaty are false, for this leader who promises to guard Israel will seek to destroy it. He tells them that "when the overflowing scourge passes through, you will be trampled down by it." Other words, when this man wages war against Israel, the nation will be destroyed by it. God elaborates on the Antichrist's deception and intention as he signed this agreement. In Psalm 55: 20-21 it says: "He has put forth his hands against those who were at peace with him: He has broken his covenant. The words of his mouth were smoother than butter, But war was in his heart; His words were softer than oil, Yet they were drawn swords"

Scripture provides a view to the emotional and physical picture of Israel once the Antichrist breaks the treaty and lays siege to the nation. Isaiah 33:7-9 states: "Surely their valiant ones shall cry outside: the ambassadors of peace shall week bitterly. The highways lie waste, the wayfaring man ceases. He has broken the covenant, he has despised the cities, he regards no man. The earth mourns and languishes; Lebanon is ashamed and shriveled: Sharon is like a wilderness: and Bashan and Carmel shake off their fruits"

Daniel 11:37 emphasizes the Antichrist's regard for no man. It states: "He shall regard neither the God of his fathers, nor the desire of women, nor regard any god: for he shall magnify himself above them all."

Genesis 3:16 teaches that Eve represented all of womanhood. Her "desire shall be for your husband." The desire of women is man. Thus, the Antichrist will regard no man.

16

THE FINAL WORLD EMPIRE AND GOD'S PROMISE

Twenty-three years ago on September 11, 1990 George Bush stood at a podium in front of congress and uttered the phrase New World Order. Like lightening, it bolted through the airwaves of conspiracy theorists and the huddled masses of Evangelical Christians. The New World Order would launch the Antichrist and the one-world government the Bible describes. New World Order became the end all, catch-all phrase of Bible Prophecy watchers. While the apostle John sat on a rock on the Isle of Patmos he saw in his end-time vision the whole world worshiping and taking the Mark of the Beast. John's vision recorded in Revelation chapter 13 aligned perfectly with a New World Order, which implied the possibility of a World state.

The New World Order is now for the history books. George Bush's, phrase hopped the conspiracy theorist bandwagon, it rocked the evangelical Christian world and was beaten into the ground and sand so many times, and now it finds itself in the dust bin of history. Bush coined the phrase 22 years ago. The Berlin wall fell and the new world order existed for about the next 20 years The new world order rose from the ashes of communism. George Bush envisioned democracy on a world wide scale with globalization bringing the nations together in cooperation. Conspiracy theorists embraced George Bush's New World Order as headed by their Illuminati's and Bilderbergers. It's been well over 20 years, and no takeover. We do not have a world governed by the conspiracy theorist's secret societies.

What happened to the New World Order and why is now a phrase and a piece of history scholars will write into history books? It transitioned to Age of Empires. We have walked through the doors to the empire Age. No one expected it, no one imagined it. The prophet Daniel talked about it and laid it out in vivid detail over 2500 years ago.

According to the words of the prophets an empire launches the Antichrist. specifically The Revived Roman Empire. As Daniel stood in front of King Nebuchadnezzar of Babylon interpreting his dream image and relating it to the end times, he forecasted and envisioned the four Empires that would rule Israel. Among them stood the Empire that the Antichrist will rise to super power prominence. Daniel never wrote about a New World Order, he foresaw an empire, which stands with the appearance of a Terminator. It walks on two enormous iron legs. This monster opens its lion like mouth and shows its great iron teeth. It crushes all who oppose it.

In 2008 MEP and former prime minister of Belgium Guy Verhofstadt named the current geopolitical frame work as the Age of Empires. He brought up the emerging BRIC nations of Brazil, Russia, India, China and the United States and European Union.
Russia has 143, million citizens,
Brazil the fifth largest nation in the world has 200 million

The United States population of 316 million is cited as the third largest nation, but is knocked off of its third place slot by the European Union, which has over 508 million citizens.
China and India are monolith. China is the largest nation in the world with 1.3 billion persons and India follows right behind with 1.21 billion.

The empire that prophecy watchers should keep an eye on, is the one that Daniel pinpoints as the final world empire. The European Union is the revived roman empire. European Union Commission President Manuel Barroso while sitting among a group of European Union officials was asked by a reporter about the structure of the European Union and he answered calmly that it is an empire. He called it a non-imperial empire.

During the cold war we lived in a bipolar world with the US and Russia as the leading superpowers. Afterwards the world went unipolar with the United States as the sole superpower. Some experts say we have evolved into a multipolar world, which has replaced the New World Order. A multipolar world will only exist for a short time. The Bible describes a unipolar world headed by an empire that unifies the world. It does not happen via a conspiracy, but rather via geopolitics. Thus, one of the empires in the multipolar world reaches the top of the list in economic strength and power turning the multipolar world, unipolar.

John while standing on the sands of the Mediterranean sea sees a beast rise up out of the sea. Its seven heads and ten horns pop out of the water and its fully exposed head bears a blasphemous name. John does not see a New World Order, he sees an empire, The final world empire rules the nations. The final world empire makes the world's citizens take the Mark of the Beast. The final world empire will write the rules for the globe. The final world empire will launch the Antichrist who will lead this government to super power status. It will also usher in the Tribulation.

George Herbert Bush's New World Order is now history and the new order is the Age of Empire or the Empire Age. Bible prophecy watchers will see the evolution of the multipolar into a unipolar with the European Union as the leading world empire. Daniel forecast a continuation of the early Roman Empire. The EU fits the description of the Empire in its later day emergence.

GOD'S PROMISE

With the certainty that the EU is the revived Roman Empire, this signifies that the start of the Tribulation is very near. Those who have accepted Jesus Christ as their personal savior will not go through the Tribulation. God takes them out of the world in the Rapture just prior to the earth's final seven years. II Thessalonians 4:14-18 tells us:

For if we believe that Jesus died and rose again, even so, God will bring with Him those who sleep in Jesus. For this, we say to you by the word of the Lord, that we who are alive and remain until the coming of the Lord will by no means precede those who are asleep. For the Lord himself will descend from heaven with a shout, with the voice of an archangel, and with the trumpet of God: and the dead in Christ will rise first: Then we who are alive and remain shall be caught up together with them in the clouds, to meet the Lord in the air: and thus we shall always be with the Lord. Therefore comfort one another with these words.

In John's vision on the Isle of Patmos, he saw a large multitude of people dressed in white robes, praising God. John asked who these people were. The angel answered him and said: *"These are the ones who come out of the great Tribulation, and washed their robes, and made them white in the blood of the Lamb"* (Rev. 7:9,13,14). Jesus also tells the church at Philadelphia, He will keep them from the hour of trial that is coming upon the whole earth. God ushered Lot and his family out of Sodom and Gomorrah before destroying the city. He commanded Noah to build the ark, rescuing his family from the flood. God brings those who have placed their faith in his Son out of the Great Tribulation. The Rapture occurs just prior to and after the sealing of the 144,000. During the Tribulation while God shakes the world with His power, He sends His messenger's. While a few will look to Him, the greater number of mankind curses God rather than turn to Him.

A major natural disaster may occur at the same time of the Rapture. Some may regard it as people disappearing into another dimension. Others may claim that aliens abducted the missing. Experts will offer their explanations of how the disappearance of these people could have happened. The Rapture will seem unremarkable to most of the world's inhabitants.

During Israel's history, God utilized the prophets to forecast calamity and judgment on Israeli kings and on the nation for turning against Him and following other gods and pagan practices. In most instances, if the king or nation repented, God changed his mind and replaced blessings for judgment. Prior to the Babylonian invasion of Israel the prophet Jeremiah spent his life warning the kings of Israel and the Israelites of the coming Babylonian captivity. In looking at the kingdom period we see that sin progressed from idolatry and worshiping pagan gods to sacrificing children to them. The Israelites torturously murdered their children by burning them in fire to the god Molech. Israel's habitual sin resulted in the Babylonian captivity and the destruction of Solomon's Temple. In the Bible, judgment always follows grievous, unrepentant sin, especially idolatry. Before God enacts His judgment, he unfailingly warns of the coming consequence.

When God judged Sodom and Gomorrah with fire and brimstone and Noah's civilization with the flood, he rescued Noah and Lot's family and warned each of them of the coming judgment. Today we have God's Word written in the Bible, which contains the books of the Prophets and the Revelation prophecy, which details the events of the Great Tribulation and the end of the world. These prophecies are your warning. The revived Roman Empire, will launch the Antichrist and usher in the Earth's final days. The European Union is the revived Roman Empire and provides evidence of the accuracy of the prophetic writings. The fulfillment of prophecy before our eyes is our warning. If we do not know Jesus Christ as our personal Savior now is the time to accept Him and if we know Him, we must make sure that each minute of our days count in the service of the Savior because as Jesus said in the Revelation, He is coming quickly.

www.ingramcontent.com/pod-product-compliance
Lightning Source LLC
Chambersburg PA
CBHW080735230426
43665CB00020B/2745